THE ULTIMATE BABY BOOMER TRIVIA AND QUIZ BOOK

Brain Boosting Questions from 1940's, 50's, 60's, 70's & 80's

<u>Welcome to The Puzzlers Vault: Baby Boomer Trivia Edition!</u>

Step back in time with this trivia game packed with jukebox hits, groovy fashions, and iconic moments from the Baby Boomer era. Whether you're a Boomer, history buff, or trivia fan, get ready for fun surprises!

<u>How to Play:</u> Pick Your Challenge: Flip through pages or choose your favorite decade.

<u>Test Your Knowledge:</u> Answer questions (A, B, C, or D) and circle your pick. Guess if you're unsure—your instincts might surprise you!

<u>Play Your Way:</u>

Solo Mode: Tackle questions alone and track your score to become trivia master.

Group Mode: Make it a game night and see who knows their Boomer trivia best!

<u>Check Answers:</u> Flip to the answer key at the back (no peeking!) to see how you did.

<u>Keep the Fun Going:</u> Each question is a mini time machine—share stories, spark conversations, and relive the magic of the Baby Boomer era.

Are you ready to unlock the vault?

Dive in and let the trivia adventure begin!

1940s: Wartime Challenges and Post-War Dreams

1940s: Culture and Entertainment

1. In 1942, which film featured the iconic line, "Here's looking at you, kid"?
   a. Citizen Kane
   b. Gone with the Wind
   c. Casablanca
   d. The Maltese Falcon

2. Who was the best-selling music artist of the 1940s, known for hits like "White Christmas"?
   a. Frank Sinatra
   b. Bing Crosby
   c. Glenn Miller
   d. Ella Fitzgerald

3. What was the first Bugs Bunny cartoon, released in 1940?
   a. Rabbit of Seville
   b. Duck Amuck
   c. A Wild Hare
   d. The Old Grey Hare

4. Which 1946 film starring James Stewart became a Christmas classic?
   a. Miracle on 34th Street
   b. It's a Wonderful Life
   c. Holiday Inn
   d. White Christmas

5. What was the name of the popular swing bandleader who disappeared during a WWII flight in 1944?
   a. Duke Ellington
   b. Benny Goodman
   c. Glenn Miller
   d. Tommy Dorsey

6. Which magazine, launched in 1944, became known for its iconic photographs and coverage of world events?
   a. Life
   b. Time
   c. Look
   d. Newsweek

7. What entertainment medium was nicknamed the "Golden Age of Radio" during the 1940s?
   a. Soap operas
   b. Radio dramas
   c. Variety shows
   d. News broadcasts

8. Which musical duo introduced "Some Enchanted Evening" in the Broadway production of *South Pacific* (1949)?
   a. Cole Porter and Irving Berlin
   b. Rodgers and Hammerstein
   c. Lerner and Loewe
   d. George and Ira Gershwin

9. Which fashion trend became popular among women during WWII due to fabric rationing?
   a. Poodle skirts
   b. Utility clothing
   c. Flapper dresses
   d. Mini skirts

10. In the 1940s, which film studio introduced the character of Bugs Bunny?
   a. Walt Disney
   b. MGM
   c. Warner Bros.
   d. Paramount

<u>**1940s: Cars**</u>

1. Which vehicle manufacturer produced the "Jeep" used by the U.S. military during WWII?
   a. Ford
   b. Willys-Overland
   c. Chrysler
   d. General Motors

2. What small, affordable car was introduced by Crosley Motors in 1946?
   a. Crosley CC
   b. Crosley Hotshot
   c. Crosley Standard
   d. Crosley Sedan

3. Which British sports car, introduced in 1948, became iconic for its sleek design?
   a. Aston Martin DB5
   b. Jaguar XK120
   c. MG TC
   d. Triumph TR2

4. What was the first car model introduced by Kaiser-Frazer in 1947?
   a. Kaiser Manhattan
   b. Kaiser Deluxe
   c. Kaiser Special
   d. Kaiser Traveler

5. Which American car company introduced the "Woody Wagon" in the 1940s?
   a. Chevrolet
   b. Ford
   c. Plymouth
   d. Dodge

6. Which luxury car brand introduced its first production vehicle, the 356 model, in 1948?
   a. Porsche
   b. Rolls-Royce
   c. BMW
   d. Mercedes-Benz

7. Which vehicle became the first to feature an automatic transmission (Hydra-Matic), introduced in the 1940s?
   a. Oldsmobile
   b. Buick
   c. Cadillac
   d. Chrysler

8. Which iconic General Motors car debuted in 1949 and was known for its innovative styling and performance?
   a. Chevrolet Bel Air
   b. Cadillac Coupe de Ville
   c. Pontiac Chieftain
   d. Buick Roadmaster

9. What type of vehicle was mass-produced at the Willow Run assembly plant during WWII?
   a. Jeep Willys MB
   b. B-24 Liberator bomber
   c. Sherman tank
   d. Dodge Power Wagon

10. Which post-war vehicle was nicknamed the "People's Car," mass-produced in Germany starting in 1945?
    a. Volkswagen Beetle
    b. BMW 328
    c. Mercedes-Benz 170V
    d. Opel Kadett

<u>1940s: Fashion</u>

1. What 2 piece swimsuit, introduced in 1946, named after a Pacific atoll where nuclear testing took place?
   a. Tankini
   b. Bikini
   c. Monokini
   d. Swimsuit Separates

2. Which French fashion designer launched the "New Look" in 1947?
   a. Coco Chanel
   b. Christian Dior
   c. Yves Saint Laurent
   d. Pierre Balmain

3. During WWII, which material was commonly used for women's stockings after silk became unavailable?
   a. Nylon
   b. Rayon
   c. Cotton
   d. Polyester

4. With rationing in the 40s, what outfit was popular for working women?
   a. Jumpsuits
   b. Utility dresses
   c. Pencil skirts
   d. Shirtwaist dresses

5. Which hat style, characterized by a broad brim and deep crown, was popular for men during the 1940s?
   a. Bowler
   b. Fedora
   c. Boater
   d. Homburg

6. Which wartime fashion accessory for women became a symbol of practicality and patriotism?
   a. Gloves
   b. Headscarves
   c. Victory pins
   d. Berets

7. What was the primary purpose of the 1942 U.S. War Production Board's "L-85" restrictions on clothing?
   a. To conserve fabric for military use
   b. To promote uniform styles
   c. To boost domestic textile production
   d. To eliminate luxury imports

8. Which iconic shoe brand introduced wedge heels for women during the 1940s?
   a. Salvatore Ferragamo
   b. Christian Louboutin
   c. Manolo Blahnik
   d. Stuart Weitzman

9. Which men's fashion item became a symbol of rebellion when paired with leather jackets during the 1940s?
   a. Bow ties
   b. T-shirts
   c. Suspenders
   d. Flat caps

10. What fabric pattern, often seen in suits and dresses, became synonymous with 1940s wartime fashion?
    a. Polka dots
    b. Gingham
    c. Houndstooth
    d. Plaid

<u>1940s: Sports</u>

1. Which iconic baseball player made his Major League Baseball
   debut in 1947, breaking the color barrier?
   a. Hank Aaron
   b. Jackie Robinson
   c. Willie Mays
   d. Satchel Paige

2. The 1940 & 1944 Olympic Games were canceled due to WWII. In
   what year did the Olympics resume?
   a. 1946
   b. 1948
   c. 1950
   d. 1952

3. In 1941, a baseball player set a record for a 56-game hitting streak
   a. Joe DiMaggio
   b. Ted Williams
   c. Lou Gehrig
   d. Stan Musial

4. What was the first African American professional basketball team
   to join a major league, playing during the 1940s?
   a. The Harlem Globetrotters
   b. The New York Rens
   c. The Chicago Studebakers
   d. The Dayton Rens

5. Which horse became the eighth Triple Crown winner in 1941?
   a. War Admiral
   b. Count Fleet
   c. Whirlaway
   d. Assault

6. Which famous boxer, known as the "Brown Bomber," served in the military during WWII but continued his career in the late 1940s?
   a. Sugar Ray Robinson
   b. Joe Louis
   c. Rocky Marciano
   d. Max Schmeling

7. In what city were the 1948 Summer Olympics, nicknamed the "Austerity Games," held?
   a. London
   b. Paris
   c. Rome
   d. Helsinki

8. What famous football team won four consecutive NFL championships from 1940 to 1943?
   a. Chicago Bears
   b. Green Bay Packers
   c. Detroit Lions
   d. Cleveland Browns

9. Who was the first woman to swim the English Channel both ways (in 1949)?
   a. Gertrude Ederle
   b. Florence Chadwick
   c. Marilyn Bell
   d. Annette Kellerman

10. In 1945, which team won the first ever NCAA Men's Basketball Tournament?
    a. University of Kentucky
    b. University of Oregon
    c. Oklahoma A&M (now Oklahoma State University)
    d. Indiana University

1. Which global conflict dominated the first half of the 1940s?
   a. World War I
   b. World War II
   c. The Korean War
   d. The Cold War

2. What document was signed on June 6, 1944, marking the Normandy invasion?
   a. Treaty of Versailles
   b. Atlantic Charter
   c. Operation Overlord orders
   d. Potsdam Agreement

3. Where did US, UK, and Soviet leaders meet in 1945 to discuss post-war Europe?
   a. Tehran Conference
   b. Yalta Conference
   c. Geneva Conference
   d. Paris Peace Conference

4. What organization was founded in 1945 to promote peace and cooperation?
   a. NATO
   b. United Nations
   c. League of Nations
   d. World Trade Organization

5. Who became US President after FDR's death in 1945?
   a. Dwight D. Eisenhower
   b. Harry S. Truman
   c. Herbert Hoover
   d. John F. Kennedy

6. What was the name of the U.S. program that provided post-war aid to Europe starting in 1948?
   a. The Marshall Plan
   b. The Truman Doctrine
   c. The Point Four Program
   d. Lend-Lease Act

7. Which event on August 6, 1945, marked the first use of atomic weapons in warfare?
   a. Attack on Pearl Harbor
   b. Hiroshima bombing
   c. Nagasaki bombing
   d. Battle of Midway

8. In 1947, what major political doctrine was announced to contain communism?
   a. Monroe Doctrine
   b. Truman Doctrine
   c. Eisenhower Doctrine
   d. Marshall Doctrine

9. Which country gained independence from Britain in 1947, leading to the partition of India and Pakistan?
   a. Ireland
   b. India
   c. South Africa
   d. Australia

10. The Nuremberg Trials (1945–1946) prosecuted leaders of which regime?
    a. Soviet Union
    b. Nazi Germany
    c. Imperial Japan
    d. Fascist Italy

1. Which popular canned meat product became a staple during WWII due to its long shelf life?
   a. Corned beef
   b. Spam
   c. Tuna
   d. Vienna sausage

2. What household appliance, introduced in the 1940s, revolutionized how families stored food?
   a. Electric oven
   b. Refrigerator
   c. Microwave oven
   d. Washing machine

3. Which famous ballpoint pen first went on sale in 1945?
   a. Parker Pen
   b. Bic Cristal
   c. Reynolds Rocket
   d. Pilot Precise

4. What popular post-war toy, first created as a naval invention, debuted in 1945?
   a. Slinky
   b. LEGO
   c. Play-Doh
   d. View-Master

5. Which technological innovation was used during WWII to detect aircraft and later adapted for weather forecasting?
   a. Radar
   b. Sonar
   c. Telegraph
   d. Radio waves

6. What fabric, invented by DuPont in the 1940s, replaced silk in many products, including women's stockings?
   a. Nylon
   b. Polyester
   c. Rayon
   d. Acrylic

7. In 1948, which fast-food chain opened its first location, setting the stage for the modern franchise model?
   a. McDonald's
   b. Burger King
   c. In-N-Out Burger
   d. White Castle

8. Which invention in 1947 laid the foundation for modern electronic devices like computers and smartphones?
   a. Transistor
   b. Microchip
   c. Vacuum tube
   d. Circuit board

9. What consumer product, heavily promoted to housewives after WWII, became synonymous with modern cleaning?
   a. Vacuum cleaner
   b. Tupperware
   c. Electric mixer
   d. Dish soap

10. What trend in the late 1940s saw the rise of suburban housing developments, epitomized by Levittown in New York?
    a. Urban renewal
    b. Mass suburbanization
    c. Public housing
    d. Rural expansion

1940s: Business and Innovation

1. Which company launched a bottled drink campaign to boost morale in WWII?
   a. Pepsi
   b. Coca-Cola
   c. RC Cola
   d. Dr Pepper

2. In 1943, who developed the first electronic computer, ENIAC?
   a. IBM
   b. Bell Labs
   c. Sperry Rand
   d. University of Pennsylvania

3. What major credit card was founded in 1949 as the first charge card?
   a. Visa
   b. Mastercard
   c. Diners Club
   d. American Express

4. Which fast-food franchise began operations in 1948, pioneering the "Speedee Service System"?
   a. McDonald's
   b. White Castle
   c. Burger King
   d. Wendy's

5. What famous fabric brand, developed by DuPont, became widely used during the 1940s for clothing and military purposes?
   a. Kevlar
   b. Nylon
   c. Polyester
   d. Spandex

6. In 1945, what company introduced the first commercial microwave oven under the brand "Radarange"?
   a. General Electric
   b. Westinghouse
   c. Raytheon
   d. Whirlpool

7. What car brand, introduced in 1948, became synonymous with affordability and reliability in post-war Europe?
   a. Volkswagen Beetle
   b. Fiat 500
   c. Renault 4CV
   d. Citroën 2CV

8. In 1942, what well-known frozen food company was founded, revolutionizing how people purchased and prepared food?
   a. Birds Eye
   b. Swanson
   c. Banquet
   d. Green Giant

9. Which publishing company launched its first paperback books in the 1940s, making literature more accessible?
   a. Penguin Books
   b. Random House
   c. HarperCollins
   d. Simon & Schuster

10. Which company introduced the first commercially successful ballpoint pen in 1945, selling for $12.50 each?
    a. Bic
    b. Parker
    c. Reynolds
    d. Pilot

1. In 1947, what was the name of the sound barrier-breaking aircraft piloted by Chuck Yeager?
   a. Spirit of St. Louis
   b. Bell X-1
   c. Boeing B-29
   d. Lockheed SR-71

2. Which Hollywood starlet became the first major celebrity to entertain U.S. troops overseas during WWII?
   a. Judy Garland
   b. Rita Hayworth
   c. Marlene Dietrich
   d. Betty Grable

3. What candy, invented in 1941, was originally sold exclusively to the U.S. military for soldiers during WWII?
   a. Skittles
   b. Reese's Pieces
   c. M&M's
   d. Snickers

4. In 1942, the Manhattan Project was launched to develop what?
   a. Space rockets
   b. The atomic bomb
   c. Radar systems
   d. Submarine technology

5. Which comic book superhero made his debut in 1941, created by psychologist William Moulton Marston?
   a. Superman
   b. Batman
   c. Wonder Woman
   d. Captain America

6. In 1945, what famous photograph captured the raising of the U.S. flag on Iwo Jima during WWII?
   a. The D-Day Landing
   b. Raising the Flag on Mount Suribachi
   c. Pearl Harbor Memorial
   d. Victory in Europe

7. Which beverage company introduced its first diet soft drink in 1949?
   a. Coca-Cola
   b. Pepsi
   c. Dr Pepper
   d. Royal Crown (RC) Cola

8. In 1948, who became the first African American to win an Oscar for acting?
   a. Sidney Poitier
   b. Lena Horne
   c. Hattie McDaniel
   d. Dorothy Dandridge

9. Which American scientist proposed the "Big Bang" theory in 1948 to explain the origins of the universe?
   a. Edwin Hubble
   b. Fred Hoyle
   c. George Gamow
   d. Albert Einstein

10. In 1949, NATO (North Atlantic Treaty Organization) was formed. How many founding member countries did it have?
    a. 10
    b. 12
    c. 14
    d. 16

<u>Did You Know - Fun Facts About the 1940s</u>

1. **The Jeep** was originally nicknamed "General Purpose Vehicle" or "G.P.," which later evolved into "Jeep."

2. **Women's roles expanded** during WWII as they took on jobs in factories, coining the term "Rosie the Riveter."

3. The **Slinky** toy was accidentally invented when a naval engineer noticed a torsion spring fall off his desk and "walk."

4. The **atomic bomb dropped on Hiroshima** was code-named "Little Boy."

5. The first **digital computer (ENIAC)**, built in 1945, weighed over 30 tons.

6. **Drive-in theaters** gained popularity in the 1940s, with the first one opening in New Jersey.

7. The **Zoot Suit Riots** in Los Angeles in 1943 were a series of conflicts between servicemen and Latino youths over fashion styles.

8. **Penicillin**, discovered in the 1920s, became widely available in the 1940s, saving countless lives during the war.

9. The **Hollywood Canteen**, opened during WWII, was a club where service members could enjoy free food and entertainment provided by stars like Bob Hope and Bette Davis.

10. **The Dead Sea Scrolls**, ancient Jewish manuscripts, were discovered in 1947 near the Dead Sea.

1950s: Rock and Roll, Suburbia, and the Space Race

1950s: Culture and Entertainment

1. Which 1952 musical featured the iconic song "Singin' in the Rain"?
   a. West Side Story
   b. The Sound of Music
   c. Singin' in the Rain
   d. An American in Paris

2. Who was crowned the "King of Rock and Roll" during the 1950s?
   a. Buddy Holly
   b. Chuck Berry
   c. Elvis Presley
   d. Little Richard

3. Which television series, starring Lucille Ball, debuted in 1951 and became a cultural phenomenon?
   a. I Love Lucy
   b. The Honeymooners
   c. Leave It to Beaver
   d. Father Knows Best

4. What popular toy, introduced in 1959, was named after the daughter of its inventor, Ruth Handler?
   a. Barbie
   b. Hula Hoop
   c. Etch A Sketch
   d. Mr. Potato Head

5. Which movie star, known for *Rebel Without a Cause*, tragically died in a car accident in 1955?
   a. James Dean
   b. Marlon Brando
   c. Montgomery Clift
   d. Paul Newman

6. What genre of music, featuring artists like Chuck Berry and Jerry
   Lee Lewis, exploded in popularity during the 1950s?
   a. Rock and roll
   b. Jazz
   c. Blues
   d. Country

7. What animated Disney film, released in 1950, featured a glass
   slipper and an iconic pumpkin carriage?
   a. Sleeping Beauty
   b. Snow White and the Seven Dwarfs
   c. Cinderella
   d. Alice in Wonderland

8. Which fashion trend became popular for women in the 1950s,
   characterized by cinched waists and full skirts?
   a. Pencil skirts
   b. Poodle skirts
   c. Miniskirts
   d. Flapper dresses

9. Who sang the hit single "Johnny B. Goode" in 1958?
   a. Elvis Presley
   b. Chuck Berry
   c. Jerry Lee Lewis
   d. Buddy Holly

10. Which epic historical drama film, released in 1959, won 11
    Academy Awards, including Best Picture?
    a. Spartacus
    b. The Ten Commandments
    c. Ben-Hur
    d. Cleopatra

1950s: Cars

1. What iconic American car, introduced in 1953, became Chevrolet's
   first sports car?
   a. Mustang
   b. Corvette
   c. Thunderbird
   d. Bel Air

2. Which European car manufacturer introduced the Mini in 1959,
   which would go on to become a design icon?
   a. Fiat
   b. Volkswagen
   c. Morris Motors
   d. Renault

3. Which luxury brand introduced the "Silver Cloud" model in 1955?
   a. Bentley
   b. Rolls-Royce
   c. Mercedes-Benz
   d. Jaguar

4. What car debuted in 1957 as the first mass-produced car with tail
   fins, setting a design trend for the era?
   a. Cadillac Eldorado
   b. Chevrolet Bel Air
   c. Plymouth Fury
   d. Dodge Custom Royal

5. Which German car, known as the "People's Car," gained global
   popularity in the 1950s due to its affordability and reliability?
   a. Volkswagen Beetle
   b. BMW 501
   c. Mercedes-Benz 190
   d. Opel Kapitän

6. What innovative feature was first offered in the 1955 Chrysler C-300, earning it the title of America's first muscle car?
   a. Turbocharged engine
   b. HEMI V8 engine
   c. Four-wheel drive
   d. Supercharger

7. In 1954, Mercedes-Benz released the 300 SL. What unique feature made this car stand out?
   a. Electric engine
   b. Gullwing doors
   c. Convertible top
   d. All-wheel drive

8. What car company released the Edsel in 1957, which is remembered as one of the biggest failures in automotive history?
   a. General Motors
   b. Ford
   c. Chrysler
   d. Studebaker

9. Which Italian automaker released the 1957 Fiat 500, often referred to as the "Cinquecento"?
   a. Alfa Romeo
   b. Fiat
   c. Maserati
   d. Ferrari

10. The 1951 Hudson Hornet dominated NASCAR races during the decade. What unique design gave it an edge?
    a. Supercharged engine
    b. Low center of gravity
    c. Aerodynamic fins
    d. Lightweight aluminum body

<u>1950s: Fashion</u>

1. What French designer is credited with popularizing the "New Look?
   a. Coco Chanel
   b. Christian Dior
   c. Yves Saint Laurent
   d. Hubert de Givenchy

2. Which American actress became a 1950s fashion icon, often seen wearing pearls and classic A-line dresses?
   a. Grace Kelly
   b. Audrey Hepburn
   c. Marilyn Monroe
   d. Elizabeth Taylor

3. What women's footwear style, known for its pointed toe and thin, high heel, became popular in the 1950s?
   a. Stilettos
   b. Wedges
   c. Mary Janes
   d. Espadrilles

4. Which innovation in textiles, first used in the 50s, revolutionized swimwear by offering greater stretch and durability?
   a. Nylon
   b. Lycra (spandex)
   c. Polyester
   d. Acrylic

5. Which British fashion model, known as the first "supermodel," rose to prominence in the 1950s?
   a. Jean Shrimpton
   b. Twiggy
   c. Suzy Parker
   d. Barbara Goalen

6. What popular men's fashion trend of the 1950s included leather jackets, white T-shirts, and jeans, epitomized by Marlon Brando?
   a. Preppy style
   b. Greaser style
   c. Ivy League style
   d. Rockabilly style

7. In the 1950s, women frequently wore fitted blouses and skirts. What undergarment was worn to create the hourglass silhouette?
   a. Corset
   b. Girdle
   c. Slip
   d. Crinoline

8. Which luxury fashion house introduced the trapeze dress in 1958?
   a. Givenchy
   b. Chanel
   c. Balenciaga
   d. Dior

9. Which item of casual menswear, first introduced by Lacoste, became popular in the 1950s for its comfort and versatility?
   a. Polo shirt
   b. Hawaiian shirt
   c. V-neck sweater
   d. Denim jacket

10. What was the name of the hairstyle that involved combing hair back and securing it with pomade, a popular choice for men in the 1950s?
    a. Ducktail
    b. Crew cut
    c. Pompadour
    d. Quiff

1950s: Sports

1. In 1954, Roger Bannister became the first person to achieve which athletic milestone?
   a. Winning four Olympic gold medals
   b. Running a sub-four-minute mile
   c. Breaking the long jump world record
   d. Completing a marathon in under two hours

2. Which baseball team famously won their first World Series in 1955 after years of heartbreak?
   a. New York Yankees
   b. Chicago Cubs
   c. Brooklyn Dodgers
   d. Boston Red Sox

3. The 1952 Summer Olympics were held in which city?
   a. Helsinki
   b. Rome
   c. Melbourne
   d. London

4. In 1958, which NFL game became known as the "Greatest Game Ever Played?

   a. The Ice Bowl
   b. NFL Championship: Colts vs. Giants
   c. First Super Bowl
   d. Packers vs. Bears Rivalry Match

5. Which female tennis player, known for her serve-and-volley style, dominated the Grand Slam tournaments of the 1950s?
   a. Margaret Court
   b. Billie Jean King
   c. Althea Gibson
   d. Maureen Connolly

6. Which African American golfer broke racial barriers by competing in the PGA Tour in 1952?
   a. Charlie Sifford
   b. Lee Elder
   c. Ted Rhodes
   d. Joe Louis

7. What team won five consecutive NBA championships between 1950 and 1954?
   a. Boston Celtics
   b. Minneapolis Lakers
   c. Philadelphia Warriors
   d. New York Knicks

8. In 1950, Formula One officially began. Who was crowned the first World Drivers' Champion?
   a. Juan Manuel Fangio
   b. Giuseppe Farina
   c. Alberto Ascari
   d. Stirling Moss

9. What notable sporting equipment, first made with synthetic materials, became widely used in the 1950s?
   a. Basketball
   b. Tennis racket strings
   c. Golf balls
   d. Baseball gloves

10. Who won the Heisman Trophy in 1956 and later became a cultural icon for playing in the NFL and acting in Western films?
    a. Paul Hornung
    b. Johnny Unitas
    c. Jim Brown
    d. Frank Gifford

1950s: Politics and World Events

1. Which war began in 1950 and involved the United Nations supporting South Korea against an invasion by North Korea?
   a. Vietnam War
   b. Korean War
   c. Gulf War
   d. Chinese Civil War

2. In 1957, the Soviet Union launched which satellite, becoming the first artificial satellite to orbit Earth?
   a. Luna 1
   b. Sputnik 1
   c. Explorer 1
   d. Vostok 1

3. What U.S. senator rose to prominence during the 1950s for leading investigations into alleged communist activities?
   a. Lyndon B. Johnson
   b. Richard Nixon
   c. Joseph McCarthy
   d. Estes Kefauver

4. In 1959, Fidel Castro led a successful revolution in which country?
   a. Nicaragua
   b. Cuba
   c. Chile
   d. Argentina

5. What major civil rights event occurred in 1955–1956, starting with Rosa Parks' refusal to give up her bus seat?
   a. March on Washington
   b. Montgomery Bus Boycott
   c. Freedom Rides
   d. Selma to Montgomery March

6. In 1956, British and French forces invaded Egypt after the nationalization of what strategic waterway?
   a. Panama Canal
   b. Suez Canal
   c. Bosporus Strait
   d. Strait of Hormuz

7. Which document, signed in 1951, established the European Coal and Steel Community, a precursor to the European Union?
   a. Maastricht Treaty
   b. Treaty of Paris
   c. Treaty of Rome
   d. Lisbon Treaty

8. Which U.S. President delivered the famous "Atoms for Peace" speech to the United Nations in 1953?
   a. Harry S. Truman
   b. Dwight D. Eisenhower
   c. John F. Kennedy
   d. Richard Nixon

9. In 1954, the Supreme Court case *Brown v. Board of Education* declared what unconstitutional?
   a. Segregation in public schools
   b. Poll taxes
   c. Literacy tests for voting
   d. Racially segregated public transportation

10. Which African country gained independence from British colonial rule in 1957, becoming the first sub-Saharan country to do so?
    a. Kenya
    b. Ghana
    c. Nigeria
    d. South Africa

<u>**1950s: Everyday Life**</u>

1. What popular suburban housing development, started in the 1950s, epitomized post-war mass-produced neighborhoods?
   a. Pleasantville
   b. Levittown
   c. Suburban Acres
   d. Green Valley

2. Which household appliance, introduced in the 1950s, became a symbol of modern kitchen convenience?
   a. Microwave oven
   b. Dishwasher
   c. Electric blender
   d. Automatic toaster

3. What board game, released in 1957, became a a family favorite?
   a. Monopoly
   b. Risk
   c. Clue
   d. Scrabble

4. Which toy, first sold in 1958, allowed children to snap together colorful plastic pieces to build structures?
   a. Tinker Toys
   b. LEGO bricks
   c. Lincoln Logs
   d. Meccano

5. What consumer trend saw the rise of diners and car hops serving food to customers in their vehicles?
   a. Fast food drive-ins
   b. Food trucks
   c. Street food vendors
   d. Casual dining chains

6. In 1954, what scientific breakthrough allowed the widespread production of antibiotics, saving millions of lives?
   a. Mass production of penicillin
   b. Discovery of insulin synthesis
   c. Development of the polio vaccine
   d. Creation of synthetic vitamins

7. What type of television programming dominated family entertainment in the 1950s, leading to the nickname "Golden Age?
   Sitcoms
   b. Variety shows
   c. News programs
   d. Game shows

8. What American automobile feature, introduced in the 1950s, became synonymous with the style and innovation of the decade?
   a. Tail fins
   b. Sunroof
   c. Seat belts
   d. Alloy wheels

9. What beverage became a household staple in the 1950s, marketed as the perfect drink for a modern, busy lifestyle?
   a. Instant coffee
   b. Soft drinks
   c. Iced tea
   d. Orange juice concentrate

10. What type of shopping venue, first popularized in the 1950s, allowed consumers to browse multiple stores under one roof?
   a. Strip mall
   b. Shopping mall
   c. Department store
   d. Farmer's market

<u>1950s: Business and Innovation</u>

1. What fast-food chain, founded in 1955, pioneered the franchise model and became a global phenomenon?
   a. Wendy's
   b. Burger King
   c. McDonald's
   d. Dairy Queen

2. In 1953, which company launched the first color television set for consumers?
   a. General Electric
   b. RCA
   c. Zenith
   d. Westinghouse

3. What business innovation, first developed in the 1950s, allowed for efficient warehousing and inventory management?
   a. Barcode
   b. Conveyor belt
   c. Pallet jack
   d. Automated stock tracking

4. Which frozen meal brand debuted in 1954?
   a. Banquet
   b. Stouffer's
   c. Swanson
   d. Birds Eye

5. What automobile innovation, introduced in the 1950s, improved highway travel safety?
   a. Seat belts
   b. Cruise control
   c. Airbags
   d. Anti-lock brakes

6. In 1957, which Japanese company released the first mass-produced electric rice cooker?
   a. Sony
   b. Toshiba
   c. Panasonic
   d. Mitsubishi

7. Which credit card, introduced in 1950, was the first to be accepted at multiple establishments?
   a. Visa
   b. Mastercard
   c. Diners Club
   d. American Express

8. What revolutionary discovery in the 1950s allowed for the development of modern computers and electronics?
   a. Microprocessor
   b. Transistor
   c. Circuit board
   d. Vacuum tube

9. Which iconic brand introduced its first sneaker, the Chuck Taylor All Star, which became a staple in the 1950s?
   a. Adidas
   b. Converse
   c. Nike
   d. Puma

10. What major economic initiative was signed into law by President Eisenhower in 1956, significantly expanding U.S. infrastructure?
    a. The Federal Aid Highway Act
    b. The Marshall Plan
    c. The Rural Electrification Act
    d. The National Defense Education Act

1. What iconic children's TV show, featuring a cowboy marionette named Howdy, premiered in 1955?
   a. *The Howdy Doody Show*
   b. *Captain Kangaroo*
   c. *Kukla, Fran, and Ollie*
   d. *Mister Rogers' Neighborhood*

2. Which U.S. Senator delivered the famous "Checkers speech"?
   Lyndon B. Johnson
   b. Richard Nixon
   c. Hubert Humphrey
   d. John F. Kennedy

3. In 1959, which Alaskan city became the last stop on the Trans-Alaska Railroad?
   a. Fairbanks
   b. Anchorage
   c. Juneau
   d. Sitka

4. What groundbreaking novel by J.D. Salinger was published in 1951, becoming a symbol of teenage rebellion?
   a. *On the Road*
   b. *The Catcher in the Rye*
   c. *To Kill a Mockingbird*
   d. *Fahrenheit 451*

5. Who gave the famous "I Have Seen the Future" speech at the 1958 World's Fair, highlighting advances in technology?
   a. Walt Disney
   b. Dwight D. Eisenhower
   c. Buckminster Fuller
   d. General Motors

6. What product, introduced in the 1950s, became the first packaged cake mix to include real frosting?
   a. Duncan Hines
   b. Pillsbury
   c. Betty Crocker
   d. Hostess

7. In 1956, Elvis Presley appeared on which TV show, famously censored from the waist down due to his dancing?
   a. *The Ed Sullivan Show*
   b. *American Bandstand*
   c. *The Tonight Show*
   d. *Your Hit Parade*

8. Which U.S. state was the first to approve the construction of a nuclear power plant in 1957?
   a. California
   b. Pennsylvania
   c. New York
   d. Illinois

9. What color television network debuted its first full-color broadcast in 1954?
   a. CBS
   b. NBC
   c. ABC
   d. PBS

10. What 1955 Walt Disney film featured the romantic spaghetti scene between two dogs?
   a. *Bambi*
   b. *Lady and the Tramp*
   c. *101 Dalmatians*
   d. *The Aristocats*

<u>Did You Know Section: Fun Facts About the 1950s</u>

1. The first **credit card**, Diners Club, was initially created to pay for restaurant bills but expanded rapidly to other businesses.

2. **Sputnik 1**, launched in 1957, was the size of a beach ball and marked the start of the Space Race.

3. The introduction of **drive-in theaters** allowed families to watch movies from their cars, a huge trend during the suburban boom.

4. The **hula hoop**, introduced in 1958 by Wham-O, sold over 25 million units in just four months.

5. The **Polio vaccine**, developed by Jonas Salk, became widely distributed in 1955, drastically reducing cases.

6. The first **theme park**, Disneyland, opened in Anaheim, California, in 1955, redefining family entertainment.

7. **Velcro** was patented in 1955, inspired by the way burrs stick to fabric.

8. The **Golden Arches** logo for McDonald's debuted in 1953, symbolizing the franchise's rapid growth.

9. In 1959, **Hawaii** became the 50th U.S. state, completing the union as we know it today.

10. The phrase **"teenager"** became widely used in the 1950s, reflecting the emerging youth culture of the decade.

1960s: Counterculture, Civil Rights, and Moon Landings

1960s: Culture and Entertainment

1. What 1964 film starring Julie Andrews and Dick Van Dyke became a family classic including song Supercalifragilisticexpialidocious"?
   a. *The Sound of Music*
   b. *Mary Poppins*
   c. *Chitty Chitty Bang Bang*
   d. *My Fair Lady*

2. Which music festival, held in 1969, became a defining symbol of the counterculture movement?
   a. Monterey Pop Festival
   b. Altamont Free Concert
   c. Isle of Wight Festival
   d. Woodstock

3. What popular television series, debuting in 1966, introduced audiences to Captain Kirk and the crew of the Starship Enterprise?
   a. *Lost in Space*
   b. *Battlestar Galactica*
   c. *Star Trek*
   d. *Doctor Who*

4. Which British fashion icon popularized the miniskirt in the 1960s?
   a. Twiggy
   b. Jean Shrimpton
   c. Mary Quant
   d. Barbara Hulanicki

5. Which groundbreaking music album by The Beatles was released in 1967, often considered one of the greatest of all time?
   a. *Rubber Soul*
   b. *Revolver*
   c. *Sgt. Pepper's Lonely Hearts Club Band*
   d. *Abbey Road*

6. What animated television series debuted in 1960 as the first prime-time cartoon show?
   a. *The Flintstones*
   b. *The Jetsons*
   c. *Scooby-Doo, Where Are You!*
   d. *Top Cat*

7. Which 1961 film adaptation, starring Natalie Wood, won 10 Academy Awards, including Best Picture?
   a. *West Side Story*
   b. *The Sound of Music*
   c. *Breakfast at Tiffany's*
   d. *Lawrence of Arabia*

8. Who hosted the late-night show *The Tonight Show* beginning in 1962, making it a cultural staple?
   a. Jack Paar
   b. Johnny Carson
   c. Steve Allen
   d. Ed Sullivan

9. What psychedelic rock band, fronted by Jim Morrison, released its debut album in 1967?
   a. The Grateful Dead
   b. The Doors
   c. Jefferson Airplane
   d. Cream

10. Which influential film released in 1968 featured a computer named HAL 9000?
   a. *Blade Runner*
   b. *2001: A Space Odyssey*
   c. *Star Wars*
   d. *The Day the Earth Stood Still*

<u>1960s: Cars</u>

1. Which American muscle car, introduced in 1964, was marketed as "the car designed to be designed by you"?
   a. Chevrolet Camaro
   b. Pontiac GTO
   c. Ford Mustang
   d. Dodge Charger

2. In 1963, what luxury car brand released the Silver Shadow, featuring a new unibody design?
   a. Jaguar
   b. Bentley
   c. Rolls-Royce
   d. Cadillac

3. What small, affordable British car, introduced in 1959, gained immense popularity in the 1960s for its compact design?
   a. Morris Mini
   b. Austin Healey
   c. Triumph Spitfire
   d. MG Midget

4. Which Italian automaker released the Miura in 1966, often considered the world's first supercar?
   a. Ferrari
   b. Lamborghini
   c. Alfa Romeo
   d. Maserati

5. What iconic VW vehicle, was nicknamed the "Hippie Van"?
   a. Volkswagen Beetle
   b. Volkswagen Microbus
   c. Volkswagen Thing
   d. Volkswagen Squareback

6. In 1967, what car model became the first to feature shoulder seat belts as standard equipment?
   a. Volvo 144
   b. Ford Falcon
   c. Chevrolet Impala
   d. Mercedes-Benz 300SL

7. What Chevrolet sports car, introduced in 1967, was designed to compete directly with the Ford Mustang?
   a. Chevrolet Corvette
   b. Chevrolet Camaro
   c. Chevrolet Chevelle
   d. Chevrolet Nova

8. Which groundbreaking safety device, first developed in the 1960s, was later mandated in cars during the 1970s?
   a. Airbags
   b. Anti-lock brakes
   c. Seat belts
   d. Collapsible steering column

9. What high-performance British sports car, introduced in 1961, was famously driven by James Bond in *Goldfinger*?
   a. Aston Martin DB5
   b. Jaguar E-Type
   c. Rolls-Royce Silver Cloud
   d. Bentley S3 Continental

10. What American car model, discontinued in 1964, became iconic due to its role in the assassination of President John F. Kennedy?
   a. Cadillac Fleetwood
   b. Lincoln Continental
   c. Ford Thunderbird
   d. Chrysler Imperial

<u>1960s: Fashion</u>

1. Which British model, known for her pixie haircut, became an icon?
   a. Jean Shrimpton
   b. Twiggy
   c. Veruschka
   d. Penelope Tree

2. What futuristic fashion trend of the 1960s was heavily influenced by the Space Race?
   a. Mod style
   b. Hippie fashion
   c. Space-age fashion
   d. Avant-garde

3. Which Italian designer introduced animal prints into mainstream fashion during the 1960s?
   a. Giorgio Armani
   b. Emilio Pucci
   c. Roberto Cavalli
   d. Valentino

4. Which iconic footwear, characterized by its knee-high length and white color, became a hallmark of the 1960s?
   a. Ballet flats
   b. Go-go boots
   c. Platform shoes
   d. Mary Janes

5. What American designer is credited with popularizing casual sportswear and the "all-American look" in the 1960s?
   a. Anne Klein
   b. Ralph Lauren
   c. Calvin Klein
   d. Halston

6. The tie-dye trend, associated with the counterculture movement, was inspired by which traditional fabric-dyeing technique?
   a. Batik
   b. Shibori
   c. Ikat
   d. Chintz

7. Which fashion capital hosted the first ready-to-wear collection in 1966, establishing the concept of "prêt-à-porter"?
   a. Paris
   b. Milan
   c. New York
   d. London

8. What hairstyle, named after a geographical location, was worn by both men and women and became a symbol of rebellion?
   a. Afro
   b. Mullet
   c. Mohawk
   d. Pompadour

9. Which Indian-inspired garment, often worn by hippies, became a popular fashion item in the 1960s?
   a. Kaftan
   b. Sari
   c. Salwar kameez
   d. Nehru jacket

10. In 1967, Yves Saint Laurent shocked the fashion world by introducing what groundbreaking women's garment?
   a. The pantsuit
   b. The wrap dress
   c. The maxi dress
   d. The trench coat

<u>**1960s: Sports**</u>

1. Who won the heavyweight title in 1964 by beating Sonny Liston?
   a. Joe Frazier
   b. George Foreman
   c. Muhammad Ali (then Cassius Clay)
   d. Floyd Patterson

2. The 1968 Summer Olympics in Mexico City saw American athletes Tommie Smith & John Carlos make what gesture on the podium?
   a. Holding up peace signs
   b. Raising clenched fists in a Black Power salute
   c. Kneeling during the national anthem
   d. Wearing black armbands

3. Which baseball player broke Babe Ruth's home run record in 1961 by hitting 61 home runs in a single season?
   a. Mickey Mantle
   b. Roger Maris
   c. Hank Aaron
   d. Willie Mays

4. What major innovation was first introduced in the 1967 NHL season, changing how games were viewed on television?
   a. Instant replay
   b. Colored jerseys for home teams
   c. The blue-line camera angle
   d. Player microphones

5. Which country dominated gymnastics at the 1968 Olympics, with Vera Caslavska winning four gold medals?
   a. Soviet Union
   b. United States
   c. Czechoslovakia
   d. East Germany

6. What notable race car driver won the Formula One World Championship five times in the 1960s?
   a. Stirling Moss
   b. Juan Manuel Fangio
   c. Jim Clark
   d. Graham Hill

7. The first Super Bowl was played in 1967 between which two teams?
   a. Green Bay Packers and Dallas Cowboys
   b. Kansas City Chiefs and Green Bay Packers
   c. New York Giants and Baltimore Colts
   d. Oakland Raiders and Chicago Bears

8. In 1969, which soccer player scored his 1,000th career goal, earning the nickname "The King of Soccer"?
   a. Diego Maradona
   b. Johan Cruyff
   c. Pelé
   d. Eusébio

9. Which American female athlete won three gold medals in track and field at the 1960 Rome Olympics?
   a. Florence Griffith Joyner
   b. Wilma Rudolph
   c. Jackie Joyner-Kersee
   d. Betty Cuthbert

10. What iconic basketball player joined the NBA in 1969, playing for the Milwaukee Bucks and later the Los Angeles Lakers?
    a. Wilt Chamberlain
    b. Bill Russell
    c. Kareem Abdul-Jabbar (then Lew Alcindor)
    d. Jerry West

1960s: Politics and World Events

1. Which President signed the 1964 Civil Rights Act?
   a. John F. Kennedy
   b. Richard Nixon
   c. Lyndon B. Johnson
   d. Harry S. Truman

2. In 1962, what major Cold War event brought the United States and the Soviet Union to the brink of nuclear war?
   a. Bay of Pigs Invasion
   b. Cuban Missile Crisis
   c. Berlin Wall construction
   d. Prague Spring

3. In 1963, Martin Luther King Jr. delivered his "I Have a Dream" speech during which historic event?
   a. Selma to Montgomery March
   b. March on Washington for Jobs and Freedom
   c. Birmingham Campaign
   d. Freedom Rides

4. What European country got independence from Belgium in 1960?
   a. Kenya
   b. Nigeria
   c. Democratic Republic of the Congo
   d. Ghana

5. What 1966 movement by Mao aimed to preserve communism?
   a. Great Leap Forward
   b. Cultural Revolution
   c. Red Scarf Movement
   d. Long March

6. In 1961, what construction project became a physical symbol of the division between East and West during the Cold War?
   a. Berlin Wall
   b. Iron Curtain
   c. Checkpoint Charlie
   d. Soviet Bloc Border

7. What agreement, signed in 1968, aimed to prevent the spread of nuclear weapons to countries without them?
   a. Strategic Arms Limitation Treaty (SALT)
   b. Nuclear Non-Proliferation Treaty (NPT)
   c. Partial Test Ban Treaty
   d. Geneva Conventions

8. In 1967, which conflict between Israel and neighboring Arab states lasted only six days but had significant geopolitical consequences?
   a. Yom Kippur War
   b. Suez Crisis
   c. Six-Day War
   d. Lebanon Crisis

9. In 1969, which U.S. Senator from Massachusetts was involved in a controversial car accident at Chappaquiddick Island?
   a. Edward "Ted" Kennedy
   b. Robert F. Kennedy
   c. George McGovern
   d. Hubert Humphrey

10. What event in 1963 marked the assassination of President John F. Kennedy, shocking the world?
   a. Ford's Theater assassination
   b. Dallas motorcade shooting
   c. Oval Office bombing attempt
   d. Palm Beach sniper attack

1960s: Everyday Life

1. Which popular doll, introduced in 1961, became a companion to Barbie and was marketed as her boyfriend?
   a. Tommy
   b. Ken
   c. Todd
   d. Steve

2. What popular snack food was first introduced in 1964, known for its "melts in your mouth, not in your hands" slogan?
   a. Reese's Pieces
   b. Pringles
   c. M&M's Peanut
   d. Doritos

3. In 1962, what retail chain was founded in Arkansas?

   a. Target
   b. Walmart
   c. Kmart
   d. Sears

4. What 1960s device let families project movies at home?
   a. Slide projector
   b. Home movie projector
   c. VCR
   d. Betamax

5. Which kitchen appliance, first mass-produced in the 1960s, revolutionized how food was prepared by electromagnetic radiation
   a. Microwave oven
   b. Electric stove
   c. Food processor
   d. Toaster oven

6. What 1965 soft drink was marketed as a "thirst quencher"?
   a. Gatorade
   b. Sprite
   c. Mountain Dew
   d. 7-Up

7. What clothing trend of the 1960s was characterized by bright, swirling patterns and vibrant colors, often associated with the counterculture movement?
   a. Tie-dye
   b. Plaid
   c. Paisley
   d. Floral prints

8. What was the name of the first handheld calculator, released in 1967?
   a. HP-35
   b. Pocketronic
   c. CalcuMatic
   d. Addiator

9. Which fast-food chain, known for its "finger-lickin' good" chicken, began franchising nationwide in the 1960s?
   a. Kentucky Fried Chicken (KFC)
   b. Chick-fil-A
   c. Popeyes
   d. Church's Chicken

10. What major lifestyle trend emerged in the 1960s as a result of suburban expansion, giving rise to planned communities?
    a. Urban renewal
    b. Suburbanization
    c. Gated neighborhoods
    d. Eco-villages

<h1 style="text-align:center"><u>1960s: Business and Innovation</u></h1>

1. Which computer company, founded in 1968 by Robert Noyce and Gordon Moore, became a pioneer in microprocessors?
   a. IBM
   b. Intel
   c. Hewlett-Packard (HP)
   d. Texas Instruments

2. What iconic brand introduced its first sneaker, the Cortez, in 1968?
   a. Adidas
   b. Nike
   c. Reebok
   d. Puma

3. What major fast-food franchise launched its "Big Mac" in 1967, which became a signature menu item?
   a. Burger King
   b. Wendy's
   c. McDonald's
   d. Dairy Queen

4. In 1960, what type of financial institution was first established in the U.S., allowing individuals to access credit for purchases?
   a. Credit union
   b. Mutual fund
   c. Credit card bank
   d. ATM network

5. What life-saving medical device, invented in 1960, revolutionized heart health by regulating heartbeat?
   a. Defibrillator
   b. Pacemaker
   c. Artificial heart valve
   d. Ventilator

6. Which beverage company introduced its diet version, "Tab," in 1963, marketed as a low-calorie option?
   a. Coca-Cola
   b. Pepsi
   c. Dr Pepper
   d. 7-Up

7. In 1965, which car manufacturer launched the Mustang Shelby GT350, a high-performance version of its iconic pony car?
   a. Ford
   b. Chevrolet
   c. Chrysler
   d. Dodge

8. Which corporation, originally founded in Japan, introduced the first commercially available portable tape player in 1963?
   a. Sony
   b. Panasonic
   c. Toshiba
   d. JVC

9. What major retail innovation was introduced in 1964, allowing stores to keep better track of inventory and sales?
   a. Point-of-sale system
   b. Barcode scanner
   c. Shopping cart with calculator
   d. Credit card reader

10. What company, known for its computers, was founded in 1966 as the precursor to the later tech giant Hewlett-Packard?
    a. Dell
    b. Digital Equipment Corporation (DEC)
    c. Compaq
    d. HP Labs

1960s: Bonus Rapid Fire Round and Did You Know

1. What iconic toy, introduced in 1963, was marketed as "an art medium for everyone"?
   a. Lite-Brite
   b. Etch A Sketch
   c. Spirograph
   d. View-Master

2. In 1969, which fast-food chain debuted its famous "Frosty" dessert?
   a. Wendy's
   b. Dairy Queen
   c. McDonald's
   d. Baskin-Robbins

3. What historical speech began with the words "One small step for man, one giant leap for mankind"?
   a. Martin Luther King Jr.'s "I Have a Dream" speech
   b. John F. Kennedy's moonshot speech
   c. Neil Armstrong's moon landing speech
   d. Lyndon B. Johnson's inaugural address

4. What iconic product, launched in 1964, promised to "change the way the world communicates"?
   a. Xerox copier
   b. Push-button telephone
   c. Fax machine
   d. Color television

5. What consumer product got mandatory warnings in 1966?
   a. Alcohol bottles
   b. Cigarette packages
   c. Sugary cereals
   d. Processed meat products

6. What groundbreaking space mission launched in 1961, making Yuri Gagarin the first human in space?
   a. Sputnik 1
   b. Vostok 1
   c. Apollo 11
   d. Gemini 3

7. Which 1967 science fiction TV show became a cult classic and spawned a decades-long franchise?
   a. *Star Trek*
   b. *Lost in Space*
   c. *The Twilight Zone*
   d. *Doctor Who*

8. What car model, introduced in 1964, became one of Ford's best-selling vehicles of all time?
   a. Mustang
   b. Thunderbird
   c. Falcon
   d. Fairlane

9. What style of architecture, known for its clean lines and futuristic shapes, gained popularity in the 1960s?
   a. Brutalism
   b. Art Deco
   c. Mid-century modern
   d. Postmodernism

10. Which iconic American music festival, held in upstate New York in 1969, symbolized the counterculture movement?
    a. Monterey Pop Festival
    b. Altamont Free Concert
    c. Woodstock
    d. Isle of Wight Festival

<u>Did You Know Section: Fun Facts About the 1960s</u>

1. The **world's first ATM** was installed in London in 1967, revolutionizing banking forever.

2. The **first heart transplant** was performed in South Africa in 1967 by Dr. Christiaan Barnard.

3. **Bell-bottoms** became a fashion trend inspired by naval uniforms, spreading widely through the counterculture movement.

4. The **Beatles' "Hey Jude"** became the longest-running #1 hit on the Billboard Hot 100 in 1968, staying at the top for nine weeks.

5. The **Smiley face** was created in 1963 as part of a marketing campaign to boost employee morale.

6. The **first Walmart** store opened in Rogers, Arkansas, in 1962, marking the start of a retail revolution.

7. **NASA's Apollo program** not only landed men on the moon but also led to the development of memory foam, now widely used in mattresses.

8. **1965 saw the birth of email**—MIT scientists sent messages between time-sharing computers.

9. The **1966 Batman TV series**, starring Adam West, sparked a superhero craze in popular culture.

10. The **Barbie Dreamhouse**, introduced in 1962, reflected the growing emphasis on suburban family life and materialism.

1970s: Disco, Détente, and Digital Beginnings

1970s: Culture and Entertainment

1. What iconic 1977 movie, directed by George Lucas, became a worldwide cultural phenomenon and launched a major franchise?
   a. *Star Trek: The Motion Picture*
   b. *Star Wars*
   c. *Close Encounters of the Third Kind*
   d. *Battlestar Galactica*

2. What genre of music, characterized by a strong beat and catchy melodies, dominated dance floors in the 1970s?
   a. Funk
   b. Disco
   c. Rock and roll
   d. Punk

3. Which TV show, debuting in 1974, followed the lives of the Ingalls family in the late 19th century Midwest?
   a. *Bonanza*
   b. *Little House on the Prairie*
   c. *The Waltons*
   d. *Gunsmoke*

4. Who became a pop culture sensation with her role in *Grease*?
   a. Debbie Reynolds
   b. Olivia Newton-John
   c. Liza Minnelli
   d. Barbara Streisand

5. What fashion trend of the 1970s featured high-waisted pants with flared bottoms?
   a. Bell-bottoms
   b. Cargo pants
   c. Jumpsuits
   d. Culottes

6. What 1976 song by Queen is often considered one of the greatest rock anthems of all time?
   a. "Bohemian Rhapsody"
   b. "We Will Rock You"
   c. "Don't Stop Me Now"
   d. "Another One Bites the Dust"

7. Which influential director won his first Academy Award for Best Picture with *The Godfather* in 1972?
   a. Francis Ford Coppola
   b. Martin Scorsese
   c. Steven Spielberg
   d. Stanley Kubrick

8. Which animated TV series, launched in 1976, became a massive hit among children and featured a group of problem-solving teenagers and their talking dog?
   a. *The Jetsons*
   b. *Scooby-Doo, Where Are You!*
   c. *The Flintstones*
   d. *Captain Caveman and the Teen Angels*

9. What 1971 John Lennon song became a peace anthem?
   a. "Give Peace a Chance"
   b. "Imagine"
   c. "Working Class Hero"
   d. "Power to the People"

10. Which 1975 film, set on a beach town terrorized by a great white shark, became one of the first summer blockbusters?
    a. *The Deep*
    b. *The Abyss*
    c. *Jaws*
    d. *The Poseidon Adventure*

<u>1970s: Cars</u>

1. Which American car, introduced in 1970, became an icon of the muscle car era with its powerful HEMI engine?
   a. Ford Mustang Boss 429
   b. Plymouth Barracuda
   c. Dodge Challenger
   d. Chevrolet Camaro Z28

2. What safety feature became mandatory in U.S. cars in 1974?
   a. Airbags
   b. Seat belts
   c. Catalytic converters
   d. Anti-lock brakes

3. What was the name of the first mass-produced electric car, launched in 1974?
   a. AMC Gremlin Electric
   b. General Motors EV1
   c. Sebring-Vanguard CitiCar
   d. Chrysler Electrovair

4. Which luxury car, produced in the 1970s, was nicknamed the "Silver Shadow" and featured advanced self-leveling suspension?
   a. Rolls-Royce Silver Shadow
   b. Cadillac Eldorado
   c. Mercedes-Benz 600
   d. Jaguar XJ12

5. In 1973, which iconic Italian sports car manufacturer released the Countach, known for its futuristic wedge design?
   a. Lamborghini
   b. Ferrari
   c. Maserati
   d. Alfa Romeo

6. What car model became a symbol of the oil crisis in the 1970s due to its exceptional fuel efficiency?
   a. Volkswagen Beetle
   b. Honda Civic
   c. Toyota Corolla
   d. Datsun 510

7. Which American compact car, launched by AMC in 1970, was advertised as "the first wide small car"?
   a. AMC Gremlin
   b. AMC Hornet
   c. AMC Pacer
   d. AMC Rebel

8. What German luxury car manufacturer introduced the 5 Series in 1972, setting a new standard for executive sedans?
   a. BMW
   b. Mercedes-Benz
   c. Audi
   d. Porsche

9. The 1977 Pontiac Firebird Trans Am became famous for its appearance in which hit film?
   a. *American Graffiti*
   b. *Smokey and the Bandit*
   c. *Grease*
   d. *Vanishing Point*

10. What vehicle type surged in popularity during the 1970s as families sought more space and comfort for road trips?
    a. Pickup trucks
    b. Minivans
    c. Station wagons
    d. SUVs

1970s: Fashion

1. Which style of pants, characterized by their wide flared legs, became a hallmark of 1970s fashion?
   a. Bell-bottoms
   b. Capri pants
   c. Jumpsuits
   d. Cargo pants

2. What 1970s footwear had thick soles and high heels?
   a. Platforms
   b. Clogs
   c. Wedges
   d. Espadrilles

3. Which French fashion designer is credited with introducing the concept of "ready-to-wear" (prêt-à-porter) in the early 1970s?
   a. Yves Saint Laurent
   b. Coco Chanel
   c. Pierre Cardin
   d. Hubert de Givenchy

4. What fabric pattern, inspired by traditional Indian designs, became trendy in the 1970s and was associated with bohemian fashion?
   a. Paisley
   b. Gingham
   c. Plaid
   d. Houndstooth

5. Which American designer, known for his minimalist style, became a major force in the fashion industry during the 1970s?
   a. Ralph Lauren
   b. Halston
   c. Calvin Klein
   d. Oscar de la Renta

6. What popular hairstyle, worn by both men and women in the 1970s, was characterized by its large, rounded, and natural appearance?
   a. Afro
   b. Mullet
   c. Pixie cut
   d. Shag

7. Which iconic fashion magazine launched its first international edition in the 1970s, marking a global expansion?
   a. Harper's Bazaar
   b. Vogue
   c. Elle
   d. Cosmopolitan

8. What garment, popularized by the disco culture of the 1970s, featured a one-piece design often with flared legs?
   a. Jumpsuit
   b. Tracksuit
   c. Bodysuit
   d. Overalls

9. What type of shirt, characterized by its brightly colored patterns and loose fit, became a staple of men's fashion in the 1970s?
   a. Polo shirt
   b. Hawaiian shirt
   c. Tunic
   d. Dashiki

10. What 1970s hippie accessory was worn on the neck or head?
   a. Bandana
   b. Beaded necklace
   c. Flower crown
   d. Scarf

<u>**1970s: Sports**</u>

1. Who beat Bobby Riggs in the 1973 "Battle of the Sexes"?

    a. Martina Navratilova
    b. Chris Evert
    c. Billie Jean King
    d. Margaret Court

2. What major sporting event debuted in 1970, becoming an annual competition between the AFC and NFC champions?
    a. The Super Bowl
    b. The Pro Bowl
    c. The NFL Playoffs
    d. The Rose Bowl

3. Which U.S. city hosted the 1976 Summer Olympics?
    a. Los Angeles
    b. Montreal
    c. New York City
    d. Moscow

4. Who became the first heavyweight boxer to win the world title three times after defeating George Foreman in the 1974 "Rumble in the Jungle"?
    a. Muhammad Ali
    b. Joe Frazier
    c. Larry Holmes
    d. Ken Norton

5. What racehorse won the Triple Crown in 1973, setting speed records in all three races that still stand today?
    a. Secretariat
    b. Seattle Slew
    c. Affirmed
    d. Sham

6. In 1972, which basketball team won Olympic gold after controversially losing the final seconds to the Soviet Union?
   a. Canada
   b. United States
   c. Yugoslavia
   d. Soviet Union

7. Which iconic Formula One driver won three world championships during the 1970s?
   a. Ayrton Senna
   b. Niki Lauda
   c. Jackie Stewart
   d. Emerson Fittipaldi

8. What MLB team won three consecutive World Series titles from 1972 to 1974?
   a. New York Yankees
   b. Oakland Athletics
   c. Cincinnati Reds
   d. Baltimore Orioles

9. In 1977, which Brazilian soccer legend played his last professional match, marking the end of an era?
   a. Zico
   b. Pelé
   c. Socrates
   d. Jairzinho

10. What women's sports organization was founded in 1972 following the passage of Title IX, promoting equality in athletics?
    a. Women's National Basketball Association (WNBA)
    b. Women's Sports Foundation
    c. National Women's Soccer League (NWSL)
    d. International Women's Athletic Federation

1970s: Politics and World Events

1. What scandal caused Nixon to resign in 1974?
   a. Watergate
   b. Iran-Contra Affair
   c. Teapot Dome Scandal
   d. Pentagon Papers

2. Which Southeast Asian country fell to communist forces in 1975, marking the end of a long conflict involving U.S. military forces?
   a. Cambodia
   b. Vietnam
   c. Laos
   d. Thailand

3. In 1979, which country experienced a revolution that replaced the Shah with an Islamic Republic led by Ayatollah Khomeini?
   a. Afghanistan
   b. Saudi Arabia
   c. Iran
   d. Pakistan

4. What international organization, founded in 1971, focused on environmental activism, including anti-whaling campaigns?
   a. Sierra Club
   b. World Wildlife Fund (WWF)
   c. Greenpeace
   d. Friends of the Earth

5. In 1972, five men broke into the Democratic National Committee headquarters, leading to what infamous investigation?
   a. Watergate Scandal
   b. COINTELPRO
   c. Pentagon Papers
   d. Iran Hostage Crisis

6. What 1975 agreement improved East-West relations during the Cold War?
   a. Helsinki Accords
   b. SALT I Treaty
   c. Camp David Accords
   d. Paris Peace Accords

7. Which African country gained independence from Portugal in 1975, following a long struggle for liberation?
   a. Angola
   b. Zimbabwe
   c. Kenya
   d. Ghana

8. In 1979, the Soviet Union invaded which country, sparking a conflict that would last for a decade?
   a. Iran
   b. Afghanistan
   c. Iraq
   d. Pakistan

9. What 1973 peace agreement ended direct U.S. military involvement in Vietnam?
   a. Geneva Convention
   b. Paris Peace Accords
   c. Camp David Agreement
   d. SALT II Treaty

10. Which U.S. president brokered the Camp David Accords in 1978, leading to peace between Egypt and Israel?
    a. Gerald Ford
    b. Jimmy Carter
    c. Richard Nixon
    d. Ronald Reagan

1970s: Everyday Life

1. What type of personal music device, introduced by Sony in 1979, revolutionized how people listened to music?
   a. Walkman
   b. Boombox
   c. Portable CD Player
   d. Cassette Recorder

2. What popular family board game, released in 1974, allowed players to buy, sell, and trade properties in a fictional universe?
   a. Risk
   b. The Game of Life
   c. Clue
   d. Monopoly

3. What 1970s sneaker brand became an athletic and fashion staple?
   a. Converse
   b. Adidas Superstar
   c. Reebok Classic
   d. Vans

4. In 1971, which fast-food chain introduced the iconic Egg McMuffin, starting the trend of breakfast-on-the-go?
   a. Burger King
   b. McDonald's
   c. Wendy's
   d. Dunkin' Donuts

5. Which home appliance, gaining popularity in the 1970s, significantly sped up cooking times using electromagnetic waves?
   a. Microwave oven
   b. Toaster oven
   c. Slow cooker
   d. Food processor

6. What gaming console, released by Atari in 1977, became a bestseller and brought video gaming into the home?
   a. Magnavox Odyssey
   b. ColecoVision
   c. Atari 2600
   d. Intellivision

7. What American fad toy of the 1970s, made from lava-like materials, became a mesmerizing home decoration?
   a. Mood Ring
   b. Lava Lamp
   c. Pet Rock
   d. Kaleidoscope

8. What type of vehicle, popularized in the 1970s, was frequently used for long road trips and featured custom interior designs?
   a. Pickup trucks
   b. Station wagons
   c. Custom vans
   d. Minivans

9. What hair-styling device, introduced in the 1970s, allowed users to achieve smooth, straight hairstyles at home?
   a. Flat iron
   b. Curling iron
   c. Hot rollers
   d. Blow dryer

10. What iconic children's educational program, featuring Big Bird and Oscar the Grouch, expanded internationally in the 1970s?
    a. *Schoolhouse Rock!*
    b. *Sesame Street*
    c. *Mister Rogers' Neighborhood*
    d. *The Electric Company*

1970s: Business and Innovation

1. Which technology company, founded by Steve Jobs and Steve Wozniak in 1976, began with the release of the Apple I computer?
   a. Microsoft
   b. Apple
   c. IBM
   d. Hewlett-Packard

2. In 1971, what coffee chain opened its first store in Seattle, WA?
   a. Starbucks
   b. Dunkin' Donuts
   c. Caribou Coffee
   d. Peet's Coffee

3. What major fast-food chain introduced the drive-thru window in 1975, revolutionizing the industry?
   a. Wendy's
   b. Burger King
   c. McDonald's
   d. Taco Bell

4. What innovative product, launched by Polaroid in 1972, allowed users to develop photos instantly?
   a. Polaroid SX-70
   b. Polaroid Land Camera
   c. Polaroid 600
   d. Polaroid OneStep

5. Which luxury fashion brand introduced its iconic interlocking "CC" logo in the 1970s?
   a. Gucci
   b. Louis Vuitton
   c. Chanel
   d. Hermès

6. In 1973, what oil-producing organization imposed an embargo, leading to a global energy crisis?
   a. OPEC (Organization of Petroleum Exporting Countries)
   b. NATO
   c. IMF
   d. World Bank

7. What home video recording format, introduced in 1975 by Sony, competed with VHS tapes?
   a. Betamax
   b. LaserDisc
   c. DVD
   d. Compact Cassette

8. Which American retail giant, known for its big-box stores, was founded in 1971 in Arkansas?
   a. Target
   b. Walmart
   c. Kmart
   d. Costco

9. What major invention by Intel in 1971, known as the 4004, laid the foundation for modern computing?
   a. The microprocessor
   b. The transistor
   c. The circuit board
   d. Random Access Memory (RAM)

10. Which international soft drink company introduced a new product, "Mountain Dew," in the 1970s?
   a. PepsiCo
   b. Coca-Cola
   c. Dr Pepper
   d. 7-Up

1970s: Bonus Rapid Fire Round and Did You Know

1. What iconic Saturday morning children's show, featuring educational songs like "Conjunction Junction," debuted in 1973?
   a. *Sesame Street*
   b. *Schoolhouse Rock!*
   c. *The Electric Company*
   d. *Reading Rainbow*

2. What 1977 movie first earned over $300 million?
   a. *Close Encounters of the Third Kind*
   b. *Jaws*
   c. *Star Wars*
   d. *The Godfather*

3. What consumer product, introduced in 1975, consisted of a smooth stone marketed as the perfect low-maintenance pet?
   a. Lava Lamp
   b. Pet Rock
   c. Mood Ring
   d. Magic 8 Ball

4. In 1974, what groundbreaking game by Gary Gygax and Dave Arneson launched the genre of role-playing games?
   a. *Risk*
   b. *Dungeons & Dragons*
   c. *The Legend of Zelda*
   d. *Monopoly*

5. Which technology company, founded by Bill Gates and Paul Allen in 1975, began with the development of BASIC software?
   a. Apple
   b. Microsoft
   c. IBM
   d. Oracle

6. In 1972, what home appliance brand introduced the first self-
cleaning oven?
   a. General Electric
   b. Whirlpool
   c. Maytag
   d. Frigidaire

7. Which women's fragrance, launched in 1977 by Yves Saint
Laurent, became a symbol of 1970s glamour?
   a. Opium
   b. Chanel No. 5
   c. White Diamonds
   d. Shalimar

8. What musical genre, originating in the Bronx during the 1970s,
combined rapping, DJing, and breakdancing?
   a. Hip-hop
   b. Funk
   c. Reggae
   d. Punk

9. In 1976, which car manufacturer introduced the Accord, a model
that became one of the best-selling cars worldwide?
   a. Toyota
   b. Honda
   c. Nissan
   d. Ford

10. What infamous blackout event occurred in 1977, leaving much of
New York City without power and sparking widespread looting?
   a. The Northeast Blackout
   b. The NYC Blackout of 1977
   c. The Great Power Outage
   d. The Eastern Grid Failure

<u>Did You Know Section: Fun Facts About the 1970s</u>

1. The **smiley face sticker**, a cultural icon, became a marketing sensation in the early 1970s.

2. The **first email** was sent in 1971 by Ray Tomlinson, marking the beginning of modern electronic communication.

3. The **Magic 8 Ball**, a popular novelty toy, became a party staple during the 1970s.

4. The **first VCRs**, released in 1971, were originally marketed for recording television shows but were prohibitively expensive for most families.

5. **Post-It Notes** were accidentally invented by 3M scientists in 1974 while attempting to create a super-strong adhesive.

6. The **Swatch Watch**, introduced in the late 1970s, started a trend of affordable, stylish wristwatches.

7. The **disco ball**, although originating in the early 20th century, became synonymous with dance culture during the 1970s.

8. The **first barcode scanner** was used in 1974 to scan a pack of Wrigley's gum at a Marsh Supermarket.

9. The **Compact Disc (CD)** was developed in the 1970s but wasn't commercially available until the 1980s.

10. The **punk rock movement**, with bands like the Sex Pistols and The Ramones, emerged as a counterculture phenomenon.

1980s: Excess, Innovation, and Global Shifts

1980s: Culture and Entertainment

1. What 1984 film, directed by Steven Spielberg, featured a young boy befriending an extraterrestrial?
   a. *Close Encounters of the Third Kind*
   b. *E.T. the Extra-Terrestrial*
   c. *The Goonies*
   d. *Star Wars: The Empire Strikes Back*

2. Which music video by Michael Jackson, released in 1983, featured groundbreaking special effects and an iconic zombie dance?
   a. "Billie Jean"
   b. "Beat It"
   c. "Thriller"
   d. "Bad"

3. What hit sitcom, debuted in '84, followed the life of the Huxtables?
   a. *Family Ties*
   b. *The Cosby Show*
   c. *Growing Pains*
   d. *Diff'rent Strokes*

4. Which 1980s fashion trend included neon colors, leg warmers, and oversized sweatshirts, inspired by aerobics culture?
   a. Preppy style
   b. Power dressing
   c. Athleisure
   d. Workout wear

5. What legendary video game character, first introduced in 1980, became one of the most recognizable icons in gaming?
   a. Donkey Kong
   b. Mario
   c. Pac-Man
   d. Sonic

6. Which American pop star was famously dubbed the "Queen of Pop" during the 1980s?
   a. Whitney Houston
   b. Madonna
   c. Janet Jackson
   d. Cyndi Lauper

7. What science-fiction movie, released in 1985, featured a time-traveling DeLorean and the phrase "Great Scott!"?
   a. *The Terminator*
   b. *Back to the Future*
   c. *Blade Runner*
   d. *Tron*

8. What 1980s toy craze featured soft-bodied dolls with unique adoption papers?
   a. My Little Pony
   b. Care Bears
   c. Cabbage Patch Kids
   d. Teddy Ruxpin

9. Which 1982 film by Ridley Scott became a cult classic for its depiction of a dystopian future and inspired cyberpunk aesthetics?
   a. *RoboCop*
   b. *Blade Runner*
   c. *The Running Man*
   d. *Escape from New York*

10. What music album, released in 1982, became the best-selling album of all time?
    a. *Like a Virgin*
    b. *Born in the U.S.A.*
    c. *Thriller*
    d. *Purple Rain*

1. What sports car, introduced in 1984 by Chevrolet, became an instant icon and marked the launch of its fourth generation?
   a. Chevrolet Camaro
   b. Chevrolet Corvette C4
   c. Pontiac Firebird
   d. Dodge Viper

2. What reliable Japanese car was a top seller in the 1980s?
   a. Toyota Corolla
   b. Honda Civic
   c. Nissan Sentra
   d. Mazda 323

3. What Italian car manufacturer released the iconic Testarossa in 1984, featuring a distinctive wide rear design?
   a. Ferrari
   b. Lamborghini
   c. Maserati
   d. Alfa Romeo

4. Which British car, infamous for its stainless steel body and gullwing doors, was featured in *Back to the Future*?
   a. Lotus Esprit
   b. Jaguar XJ6
   c. Aston Martin V8 Vantage
   d. DeLorean DMC-12

5. In 1982, what German car manufacturer introduced the 190 series, later dubbed the "Baby Benz"?
   a. BMW
   b. Mercedes-Benz
   c. Audi
   d. Volkswagen

6. What American car brand released the Chrysler Minivan in 1984, creating an entirely new vehicle category?
   a. Dodge
   b. Ford
   c. Chrysler
   d. Chevrolet

7. Which luxury car, introduced in 1989, marked Toyota's debut into the high-end automotive market?
   a. Acura Legend
   b. Lexus LS400
   c. Infiniti Q45
   d. Mazda Millenia

8. What innovative feature, introduced in the 1980s, became a staple for car dashboards, helping drivers navigate unfamiliar roads?
   a. Cruise control
   b. GPS navigation system
   c. Digital speedometer
   d. Rearview cameras

9. Which Japanese sports car, introduced in 1986, became famous for its rotary engine and sleek design?
   a. Mazda RX-7
   b. Toyota Supra
   c. Nissan 300ZX
   d. Mitsubishi Starion

10. What American muscle car, discontinued in 1989, is remembered as a 1980s icon for its power and aggressive styling?
   a. Pontiac Trans Am
   b. Ford Thunderbird
   c. Chevrolet Monte Carlo SS
   d. Buick Grand National

1980s: Fashion

1. What 1980s fashion featured shoulder pads & oversized blazers?
   a. Preppy style
   b. Power dressing
   c. Athleisure
   d. Bohemian chic

2. What iconic footwear brand, originally designed for basketball, became a staple of 1980s street fashion?
   a. Adidas Superstar
   b. Nike Air Jordans
   c. Converse Chuck Taylor
   d. Reebok Pumps

3. Which French designer, known for his avant-garde creations, popularized the "cone bra" worn by Madonna?
   a. Jean Paul Gaultier
   b. Yves Saint Laurent
   c. Thierry Mugler
   d. Pierre Cardin

4. What fabric, characterized by its shiny and stretchy texture, became synonymous with 1980s workout wear?
   a. Lycra (spandex)
   b. Polyester
   c. Rayon
   d. Nylon

5. Which hairstyle, popular among men and women in the 1980s, was described as "business in the front, party in the back"?
   a. Mullet
   b. Perm
   c. Mohawk
   d. Shag

6. What British pop culture figure became a fashion icon for her colorful, punk-inspired looks during the 1980s?
   a. Siouxsie Sioux
   b. Cyndi Lauper
   c. Boy George
   d. Annie Lennox

7. Which American fashion brand, known for its colorful polo shirts, embodied preppy style in the 1980s?
   a. Tommy Hilfiger
   b. Ralph Lauren
   c. Calvin Klein
   d. Lacoste

8. What accessory, often made of neon plastic, became a popular item for keeping hair in place during the 1980s?
   a. Headbands
   b. Scrunchies
   c. Barrettes
   d. Hair claws

9. Which fashion designer created the iconic safety pin dress worn by Elizabeth Hurley in the late 1980s?
   a. Gianni Versace
   b. Giorgio Armani
   c. Alexander McQueen
   d. Christian Lacroix

10. What 1980s trend saw young people wearing acid-wash denim jackets and jeans?
   a. Grunge
   b. Rocker style
   c. Punk
   d. New Romantic

<u>1980s: Sports</u>

1. Who did the U.S. hockey team beat in the 1980 "Miracle on Ice"?
   a. Canada
   b. Soviet Union
   c. Finland
   d. Sweden

2. Which tennis player won all four Grand Slam titles in 1988, completing the Golden Slam by also winning Olympic gold?
   a. Steffi Graf
   b. Martina Navratilova
   c. Chris Evert
   d. Monica Seles

3. What professional basketball player, known as "His Airness," was drafted by the Chicago Bulls in 1984?
   a. Magic Johnson
   b. Michael Jordan
   c. Larry Bird
   d. Charles Barkley

4. In 1987, what famous boxing match ended in just 91 seconds when Mike Tyson defeated his opponent?
   a. Tyson vs. Holyfield
   b. Tyson vs. Spinks
   c. Tyson vs. Lewis
   d. Tyson vs. Ruddock

5. Which Olympic sprinter, nicknamed "Flo-Jo," set world records in the 100m and 200m that still stand today?
   a. Marion Jones
   b. Florence Griffith Joyner
   c. Jackie Joyner-Kersee
   d. Gail Devers

6. Which Major League Baseball team broke their 86-year championship drought by winning the 1986 World Series?
    a. Boston Red Sox
    b. New York Mets
    c. Los Angeles Dodgers
    d. St. Louis Cardinals

7. What professional wrestler, known as "The Hulkster," became a household name and a cultural phenomenon in the 1980s?
    a. Randy Savage
    b. Hulk Hogan
    c. Andre the Giant
    d. Ric Flair

8. What F1 driver won his first title in 1989?
    a. Ayrton Senna
    b. Alain Prost
    c. Nigel Mansell
    d. Nelson Piquet

9. What U.S. city hosted the 1984 Summer Olympics, marking a financial success despite the boycott by several Eastern Bloc countries?
    a. Atlanta
    b. Los Angeles
    c. New York
    d. Chicago

10. Which soccer legend led Argentina to victory in the 1986 FIFA World Cup, famously scoring the "Hand of God" goal?
    a. Pelé
    b. Diego Maradona
    c. Johan Cruyff
    d. Zico

1980s: Politics and World Events

1. Which U.S. President, known for his economic policies and anti-Soviet rhetoric, served two terms during the 1980s?
   a. Jimmy Carter
   b. Ronald Reagan
   c. George H. W. Bush
   d. Gerald Ford

2. What event in Berlin in 1989 symbolized the end of the Cold War?
   a. Fall of the Berlin Wall
   b. Signing of the INF Treaty
   c. Reunification of Germany
   d. Collapse of the Soviet Union

3. In 1980, which Middle Eastern country was invaded by Iraq, leading to an eight-year war?
   a. Saudi Arabia
   b. Iran
   c. Kuwait
   d. Afghanistan

4. What movement in Poland, led by Lech Wałęsa, gained international attention and challenged Soviet influence in the 80s?
   a. Glasnost
   b. Solidarity
   c. Velvet Revolution
   d. Perestroika

5. In 1986, the space shuttle *Challenger* tragically exploded shortly after takeoff. How many crew members lost their lives?
   a. Five
   b. Six
   c. Seven
   d. Eight

6. Which 1985 event, organized by Bob Geldof and Midge Ure, brought musicians together to raise funds for famine relief in Africa?
    a. Farm Aid
    b. Live Aid
    c. Band Aid
    d. Hands Across America

7. What 1986 nuclear disaster caused widespread contamination?
    a. Chernobyl
    b. Three Mile Island
    c. Fukushima
    d. Windscale Fire

8. Which reform policy, introduced by Soviet leader Mikhail Gorbachev, aimed to increase transparency in the government?
    a. Perestroika
    b. Glasnost
    c. Détente
    d. New Economic Policy

9. What African leader was imprisoned for 27 years and became a global symbol of resistance against apartheid?
    a. Nelson Mandela
    b. Desmond Tutu
    c. Steve Biko
    d. Robert Mugabe

10. In 1982, what conflict occurred between the United Kingdom and Argentina over a group of islands in the South Atlantic?
    a. Falklands War
    b. Suez Crisis
    c. Gulf War
    d. Boer War

1980s: Everyday Life

1. What revolutionary computer, introduced by Apple in 1984,
   featured a graphical user interface and a mouse?
   a. IBM PC
   b. Apple Macintosh
   c. Commodore 64
   d. Atari ST

2. In 1981, what portable gadget introduced by Sony became a global
   sensation for listening to music on the go?
   a. Walkman
   b. Discman
   c. Boom Box
   d. iPod

3. Which snack, introduced in the 1980s, became famous for its
   slogan, "Once you pop, you can't stop"?
   a. Pringles
   b. Doritos
   c. Cheetos
   d. Combos

4. What 1980s Nintendo game introduced Jumpman, later called
   Mario?
   a. Pac-Man
   b. Space Invaders
   c. Donkey Kong
   d. Galaga

5. What 1980s accessory featured vibrant braided designs?
   a. Friendship bracelets
   b. Slap bracelets
   c. Scrunchies
   d. Charm necklaces

6. What home computer system, introduced in the 1980s, became one of the best-selling PCs due to its affordability and compatibility with video games?
   a. Apple II
   b. Commodore 64
   c. IBM PC Jr.
   d. Amiga 500

7. What home gaming console, released in 1985, revitalized the video game industry after the crash of 1983?
   a. Sega Genesis
   b. Nintendo Entertainment System (NES)
   c. Atari 2600
   d. ColecoVision

8. What colorful 1980s cereal featured a naval-themed mascot?
   a. Cap'n Crunch's Peanut Butter Crunch
   b. Trix
   c. Lucky Charms
   d. Fruity Pebbles

9. What iconic children's toy line, launched in the 1980s, featured tiny homes, shops, and characters that fit in your pocket?
   a. Polly Pocket
   b. My Little Pony
   c. Littlest Pet Shop
   d. Fisher-Price Little People

10. What workout video series, launched by Jane Fonda in the 1980s, sparked a global fitness craze?
   a. Tae Bo
   b. Jazzercise
   c. Jane Fonda's Workout
   d. Sweatin' to the Oldies

1980s: Business and Innovation

1. What company launched Windows in 1985?
   a. Apple
   b. Microsoft
   c. IBM
   d. Xerox

2. What fast-food chain launched the McChicken sandwich in 1980 to compete in the growing poultry market?
   a. Burger King
   b. KFC
   c. McDonald's
   d. Wendy's

3. In 1983, what telecommunications company was broken up into smaller regional companies due to antitrust rulings?
   a. Bell Telephone Company
   b. AT&T
   c. Verizon
   d. Sprint

4. Which innovative handheld device, introduced by Casio in 1980, combined a watch with a calculator?
   a. Casio Data Bank
   b. Casio G-Shock
   c. Casio Calculator Watch
   d. Casio Wrist Tech

5. What global delivery service, famous for its overnight shipping promise, expanded internationally in the 1980s?
   a. DHL
   b. UPS
   c. FedEx
   d. USPS

6. What luxury car manufacturer, launched in 1989, was Toyota's entry into the high-end automotive market?
   a. Infiniti
   b. Acura
   c. Lexus
   d. Genesis

7. In 1982, which beverage company introduced Diet Coke, the first major brand extension of its flagship product?
   a. PepsiCo
   b. Coca-Cola
   c. Dr Pepper
   d. 7-Up

8. Which electronics company released the first compact disc (CD) player in 1982, revolutionizing how people listened to music?
   a. Sony
   b. Panasonic
   c. Philips
   d. Sharp

9. What business innovation, introduced by American Express in 1984, allowed frequent flyers to earn rewards for travel spending?
   a. SkyMiles
   b. MileagePlus
   c. Frequent Flyer Program
   d. Membership Rewards

10. Which iconic sneaker, launched in 1985, was banned by the NBA for not meeting uniform rules but became a bestseller?
   a. Reebok Pumps
   b. Nike Air Jordans
   c. Converse Chuck Taylors
   d. Adidas Superstar

<u>**1980s: Bonus Rapid Fire Round and Did You Know**</u>

1. What popular video game, created by a Russian programmer in 1984, involved fitting falling blocks into a grid?
   a. *Tetris*
   b. *Pong*
   c. *Donkey Kong*
   d. *Space Invaders*

2. Which company, founded in 1984 by Michael Dell, became a major player in the personal computer market?
   a. Gateway
   b. Dell
   c. Compaq
   d. IBM

3. In 1985, which world-famous event brought together musicians like Queen and U2 to raise funds for famine relief in Ethiopia?
   a. Farm Aid
   b. Band Aid
   c. Live Aid
   d. Hands Across America

4. Which 1980s novelty toy featured a colorful cube with rotating squares and became a global craze?
   a. Simon
   b. Rubik's Cube
   c. Etch A Sketch
   d. Magic 8 Ball

5. What luxury brand launched Obsession perfume in 1985?
   a. Ralph Lauren
   b. Calvin Klein
   c. Giorgio Armani
   d. Yves Saint Laurent

6. Which U.S. President survived an assassination attempt in 1981, famously quipping to his wife, "Honey, I forgot to duck"?
   a. Jimmy Carter
   b. Ronald Reagan
   c. George H. W. Bush
   d. Gerald Ford

7. What global electronics company introduced the Game Boy handheld console in 1989?
   a. Atari
   b. Sega
   c. Nintendo
   d. Sony

8. In 1986, which iconic American landmark celebrated its 100th anniversary with a major restoration?
   a. Mount Rushmore
   b. The White House
   c. Statue of Liberty
   d. Golden Gate Bridge

9. Which 1980s arcade game, featuring ghosts named Blinky, Pinky, Inky, and Clyde, became one of the most popular games of all time?
   a. Pac-Man
   b. Ms. Pac-Man
   c. Frogger
   d. Galaga

10. What 1985 soft drink flopped and was discontinued?
    a. Crystal Pepsi
    b. New Coke
    c. Diet Pepsi
    d. Cherry Coca-Cola

Did You Know Section: Fun Facts About the 1980s

1. **The Berlin Wall graffiti** was a form of protest art that gained significant international attention before its fall in 1989.

2. The **first cell phones**, introduced in the 1980s, cost nearly $4,000 and were the size of a brick.

3. **MTV**, which debuted in 1981, revolutionized music promotion and created iconic video moments for artists like Madonna and Michael Jackson.

4. **The Cabbage Patch Kids doll craze** led to near riots in stores during the holiday seasons of the mid-1980s.

5. The **Compact Disc (CD)** was developed jointly by Sony and Philips, with the first album released on CD being Billy Joel's *52nd Street*.

6. The **AIDS epidemic**, first recognized in the early 1980s, led to global awareness campaigns and significant scientific research.

7. **"We Are the World"**, released in 1985, brought together artists like Michael Jackson and Lionel Richie to raise funds for famine relief.

8. The **VHS vs. Betamax battle** ended with VHS dominating the home video market, despite Betamax being the technically superior format.

9. **"Top Gun"**, released in 1986, boosted U.S. Navy recruitment by 500% and cemented Tom Cruise as a Hollywood icon.

10. The **Personal Computer Revolution** in the 1980s paved the way for tech giants like Microsoft and Apple to dominate the industry.

ANSWERS

1940s

Culture & Entertainment
Answers

1. c. Casablanca
2. b. Bing Crosby
3. c. A Wild Hare
4. b. It's a Wonderful Life
5. c. Glenn Miller
6. a. Life
7. b. Radio dramas
8. b. Rodgers and Hammerstein
9. b. Utility clothing
10. c. Warner Bros.

Sources:

- IMDb.com (for film and entertainment history)
- Smithsonianmag.com (culture of the 1940s)
- Britannica.com (radio and music trends)
- History.com (fashion and wartime culture)

1940s: Cars

Answers:

1. b. Willys-Overland
2. a. Crosley CC
3. b. Jaguar XK120
4. c. Kaiser Special
5. b. Ford
6. a. Porsche
7. a. Oldsmobile
8. b. Cadillac Coupe de Ville
9. b. B-24 Liberator bomber
10. a. Volkswagen Beetle

Sources:

- Smithsonianmag.com (wartime vehicle production and post-war innovations)
- Hotrod.com (iconic cars of the 1940s)
- Britannica.com (historical overview of car manufacturing)
- History.com (impact of WWII on car production)

1940s: Fashion

Answers

1. b. Bikini
2. b. Christian Dior
3. a. Nylon
4. b. Utility dresses
5. b. Fedora
6. b. Headscarves
7. a. To conserve fabric for military use
8. a. Salvatore Ferragamo
9. b. T-shirts
10. d. Plaid

Sources:

- Vogue.com (wartime and post-war fashion trends)
- Smithsonianmag.com (impact of WWII on clothing)
- Britannica.com (evolution of fashion in the 1940s)
- Chanel.com (luxury and designer history)

1940s: Sports

Answers

1. b. Jackie Robinson
2. b. 1948
3. a. Joe DiMaggio
4. c. The Chicago Studebakers
5. c. Whirlaway
6. b. Joe Louis

7. a. London
8. a. Chicago Bears
9. b. Florence Chadwick
10. c. Oklahoma A&M (now Oklahoma State University)

Sources:

- Baseballhall.org (for Jackie Robinson and Joe DiMaggio)
- Olympics.com (1948 Olympic details)
- History.com (sports during wartime)
- Britannica.com (athletes and events of the 1940s)
- Teamusa.org (Florence Chadwick and Olympic Games history)

1940s: Politics and World Events

Answers

1. b. World War II
2. c. Operation Overlord orders
3. b. Yalta Conference
4. b. United Nations
5. b. Harry S. Truman
6. a. The Marshall Plan
7. b. Hiroshima bombing
8. b. Truman Doctrine
9. b. India
10. b. Nazi Germany

Sources:

- History.com (key events of World War II and post-war politics)
- Whitehouse.gov (U.S. presidents and political doctrines)
- Britannica.com (Marshall Plan, United Nations, and Nuremberg Trials)
- Nobelpeacecenter.org (global peace movements and initiatives)

1940s: Everyday Life

Answers:

1. b. Spam
2. b. Refrigerator
3. c. Reynolds Rocket
4. a. Slinky
5. a. Radar
6. a. Nylon
7. c. In-N-Out Burger
8. a. Transistor
9. b. Tupperware
10. b. Mass suburbanization

Sources:

- Smithsonianmag.com (consumer products and technological innovations of the 1940s)
- History.com (impact of WWII on daily life and technology)
- Britannica.com (advancements in household goods and trends)
- Memory.loc.gov (post-war suburbanization and consumer culture)

1940s: Business and Innovation

Answers and Sources:

1. b. Coca-Cola
2. d. University of Pennsylvania
3. c. Diners Club
4. a. McDonald's
5. b. Nylon
6. c. Raytheon
7. a. Volkswagen Beetle
8. a. Birds Eye
9. a. Penguin Books
10. c. Reynolds

Sources:

- History.com (WWII and post-war business innovations)
- Britannica.com (inventions and consumer trends of the 1940s)

- Smithsonianmag.com (iconic brands and wartime industry adaptations)
- Memory.loc.gov (technological advancements and economic milestones)

Bonus Round Answers:

1. b. Bell X-1
2. c. Marlene Dietrich
3. c. M&M's
4. b. The atomic bomb
5. c. Wonder Woman
6. b. Raising the Flag on Mount Suribachi
7. d. Royal Crown (RC) Cola
8. c. Hattie McDaniel
9. c. George Gamow
10.   b. 12

Sources:

- History.com (major WWII and post-war developments)
- Britannica.com (cultural and scientific milestones of the 1940s)
- Smithsonianmag.com (fun facts about wartime innovations)
- Nobelpeacecenter.org (NATO formation and global diplomacy)

<u>1950's</u>

1950s: Culture and Entertainment

Answers

1. c. Singin' in the Rain
2. c. Elvis Presley
3. a. I Love Lucy
4. a. Barbie
5. a. James Dean
6. a. Rock and roll
7. c. Cinderella

8. b. Poodle skirts
9. b. Chuck Berry
10.c. Ben-Hur

Sources:

- IMDb.com (films, TV shows, and actors of the 1950s)
- Rollingstone.com (music and cultural milestones)
- Britannica.com (fashion trends and cultural shifts)
- History.com (toys and innovations of the 1950s)

1950s: Cars

Answers:

1. b. Corvette
2. c. Morris Motors
3. b. Rolls-Royce
4. a. Cadillac Eldorado
5. a. Volkswagen Beetle
6. b. HEMI V8 engine
7. b. Gullwing doors
8. b. Ford
9. b. Fiat
10.b. Low center of gravity

Sources:

- Hotrod.com (classic cars of the 1950s)
- Smithsonianmag.com (automotive design innovations)
- Britannica.com (global automotive history)
- History.com (notable cars and trends of the 1950s)

1950s: Fashion

Answers:

1. b. Christian Dior
2. a. Grace Kelly
3. a. Stilettos
4. b. Lycra (spandex)

5. d. Barbara Goalen
6. b. Greaser style
7. b. Girdle
8. d. Dior
9. a. Polo shirt
10. a. Ducktail

Sources:

- Vogue.com (fashion trends and icons of the 1950s)
- Smithsonianmag.com (textile and design innovations)
- Britannica.com (global influence of 1950s fashion)
- Chanel.com (luxury fashion and designer innovations)

1950s: Sports

Answers:

1. b. Running a sub-four-minute mile
2. c. Brooklyn Dodgers
3. a. Helsinki
4. b. NFL Championship: Colts vs. Giants
5. d. Maureen Connolly
6. a. Charlie Sifford
7. b. Minneapolis Lakers
8. b. Giuseppe Farina
9. c. Golf balls
10. a. Paul Hornung

Sources:

- Olympics.com (1952 Helsinki Games and athletic achievements)
- Baseballhall.org (Brooklyn Dodgers and baseball milestones)
- Formula1.com (early F1 championships)
- Pgatour.com (golf history and notable players)
- History.com (football and basketball in the 1950s)

1950s: Politics and World Events

Answers

1. b. Korean War
2. b. Sputnik 1
3. c. Joseph McCarthy
4. b. Cuba
5. b. Montgomery Bus Boycott
6. b. Suez Canal
7. b. Treaty of Paris
8. b. Dwight D. Eisenhower
9. a. Segregation in public schools
10. b. Ghana

Sources:

- History.com (Korean War, Sputnik, McCarthyism, and civil rights movements)
- Britannica.com (global political events of the 1950s)
- Nobelpeacecenter.org (UN speeches and international treaties)
- Naacp.org (civil rights milestones)

1950s: Everyday Life

Answers

1. b. Levittown
2. a. Microwave oven
3. b. Risk
4. b. LEGO bricks
5. a. Fast food drive-ins
6. c. Development of the polio vaccine
7. b. Variety shows
8. a. Tail fins
9. a. Instant coffee
10. b. Shopping mall

Sources:

- History.com (post-war consumer trends and technological advancements)
- Smithsonianmag.com (toys and household products of the 1950s)

- Britannica.com (Golden Age of Television and innovations)
- Memory.loc.gov (everyday life in suburban America)

1950s: Business and Innovation

Answers:

1. c. McDonald's
2. b. RCA
3. a. Barcode
4. c. Swanson
5. a. Seat belts
6. b. Toshiba
7. c. Diners Club
8. b. Transistor
9. b. Converse
10. a. The Federal Aid Highway Act

Sources:

- History.com (economic milestones and fast-food history)
- Britannica.com (technological innovations of the 1950s)
- Smithsonianmag.com (consumer products and business breakthroughs)
- Memory.loc.gov (post-war infrastructure and consumer trends)

Bonus Round Answers:

1. a. *The Howdy Doody Show*
2. b. Richard Nixon
3. a. Fairbanks
4. b. *The Catcher in the Rye*
5. d. General Motors
6. c. Betty Crocker
7. a. *The Ed Sullivan Show*
8. b. Pennsylvania
9. b. NBC
10. b. *Lady and the Tramp*

Sources:

- History.com (entertainment milestones and political events)
- Smithsonianmag.com (innovations and pop culture facts)
- Britannica.com (1950s cultural shifts and technological advancements)
- Nobelpeacecenter.org (international milestones and global trends)

1960s:

1960s: Culture and Entertainment

Answers:

1. b. *Mary Poppins*
2. d. Woodstock
3. c. *Star Trek*
4. c. Mary Quant
5. c. *Sgt. Pepper's Lonely Hearts Club Band*
6. a. *The Flintstones*
7. a. *West Side Story*
8. b. Johnny Carson
9. b. The Doors
10. b. *2001: A Space Odyssey*

Sources:

- IMDb.com (movies and television of the 1960s)
- Rollingstone.com (music milestones)
- Vogue.com (fashion of the 1960s)
- Britannica.com (cultural history and notable events)

1960s: Cars

Answers and Sources:

1. c. Ford Mustang
2. c. Rolls-Royce
3. a. Morris Mini
4. b. Lamborghini

5. b. Volkswagen Microbus
6. a. Volvo 144
7. b. Chevrolet Camaro
8. a. Airbags
9. a. Aston Martin DB5
10.b. Lincoln Continental

Sources:

- Hotrod.com (muscle cars and innovations)
- Britannica.com (automotive milestones of the 1960s)
- History.com (counterculture movement and car culture)
- Smithsonianmag.com (safety and design innovations in cars)

1960s: Fashion

Answers:

1. b. Twiggy
2. c. Space-age fashion
3. c. Roberto Cavalli
4. b. Go-go boots
5. d. Halston
6. b. Shibori
7. a. Paris
8. a. Afro
9. d. Nehru jacket
10. a. The pantsuit

Sources:

- Vogue.com (1960s fashion trends and icons)
- Smithsonianmag.com (influence of cultural movements on fashion)
- Britannica.com (international design and prêt-à-porter history)
- Chanel.com (luxury fashion innovations of the 1960s)

1960s: Sports

Answers:

1. c. Muhammad Ali (then Cassius Clay)
2. b. Raising clenched fists in a Black Power salute
3. b. Roger Maris
4. a. Instant replay
5. c. Czechoslovakia
6. c. Jim Clark
7. b. Kansas City Chiefs and Green Bay Packers
8. c. Pelé
9. b. Wilma Rudolph
10. c. Kareem Abdul-Jabbar (then Lew Alcindor)

Sources:

- Olympics.com (1968 Mexico City Games and Wilma Rudolph's achievements)
- Pgatour.com (major sports innovations and events)
- Formula1.com (F1 champions of the 1960s)
- History.com (Super Bowl I and Muhammad Ali's rise)
- Baseballhall.org (Roger Maris and baseball milestones)

1960s: Politics and World Events

Answers:

1. c. Lyndon B. Johnson
2. b. Cuban Missile Crisis
3. b. March on Washington for Jobs and Freedom
4. c. Democratic Republic of the Congo
5. b. Cultural Revolution
6. a. Berlin Wall
7. b. Nuclear Non-Proliferation Treaty (NPT)
8. c. Six-Day War
9. a. Edward "Ted" Kennedy
10. b. Dallas motorcade shooting

Sources:

- History.com (Civil Rights Act, Cuban Missile Crisis, and JFK assassination)
- Britannica.com (Cold War events and international treaties)

- Naacp.org (civil rights movement)
- Nobelpeacecenter.org (global political milestones)

1960s: Everyday Life

Answers:

1. b. Ken
2. c. M&M's Peanut
3. b. Walmart
4. b. Home movie projector
5. a. Microwave oven
6. a. Gatorade
7. a. Tie-dye
8. b. Pocketronic
9. a. Kentucky Fried Chicken (KFC)
10. b. Suburbanization

Sources:

- History.com (consumer trends and technological advances)
- Smithsonianmag.com (innovative products of the 1960s)
- Britannica.com (cultural shifts in suburban America)
- Memory.loc.gov (expansion of suburban living and consumerism)

1960s: Business and Innovation

Answers:

1. b. Intel
2. b. Nike
3. c. McDonald's
4. c. Credit card bank
5. b. Pacemaker
6. a. Coca-Cola

7. a. Ford
8. a. Sony
9. b. Barcode scanner
10. b. Digital Equipment Corporation (DEC)

Sources:

- History.com (business and economic trends of the 1960s)
- Britannica.com (technological innovations and inventions)
- Smithsonianmag.com (consumer products and brand milestones)
- Nobelpeacecenter.org (global economic milestones)

Bonus Round Answers:

1. b. Etch A Sketch
2. a. Wendy's
3. c. Neil Armstrong's moon landing speech
4. b. Push-button telephone
5. b. Cigarette packages
6. b. Vostok 1
7. a. *Star Trek*
8. a. Mustang
9. c. Mid-century modern
10. c. Woodstock

Sources:

- History.com (space exploration, moon landing, and 1960s inventions)
- Britannica.com (architectural styles and consumer trends)
- Smithsonianmag.com (pop culture and technological advances)
- Rollingstone.com (Woodstock and music history)

1970s:

Answers and Sources:

1. b. *Star Wars*
2. b. Disco
3. b. *Little House on the Prairie*
4. b. Olivia Newton-John
5. a. Bell-bottoms
6. a. "Bohemian Rhapsody"
7. a. Francis Ford Coppola
8. b. *Scooby-Doo, Where Are You!*
9. b. "Imagine"
10. c. *Jaws*

Sources:

- IMDb.com (movies and television of the 1970s)
- Rollingstone.com (music and cultural milestones)
- Vogue.com (fashion trends of the 1970s)
- Britannica.com (cultural history of the 1970s)

1970s: Cars

Answers:

1. c. Dodge Challenger
2. b. Seat belts
3. c. Sebring-Vanguard CitiCar
4. a. Rolls-Royce Silver Shadow
5. a. Lamborghini
6. b. Honda Civic
7. c. AMC Pacer
8. a. BMW
9. b. *Smokey and the Bandit*
10.   c. Station wagons

Sources:

- Hotrod.com (muscle cars and performance vehicles of the 1970s)
- Smithsonianmag.com (automotive innovations)
- Britannica.com (fuel-efficient cars during the oil crisis)
- History.com (impact of the oil crisis on car culture)

1970s: Fashion

Answers and Sources:

1. a. Bell-bottoms
2. a. Platforms
3. a. Yves Saint Laurent
4. a. Paisley
5. b. Halston
6. a. Afro
7. b. Vogue
8. a. Jumpsuit
9. d. Dashiki
10. a. Bandana

Sources:

- Vogue.com (fashion trends and designers of the 1970s)
- Britannica.com (global influence of 1970s fashion)
- Smithsonianmag.com (cultural impact on fashion)
- History.com (counterculture and disco fashion movements)

1970s: Sports

Answers:

1. c. Billie Jean King
2. a. The Super Bowl
3. b. Montreal
4. a. Muhammad Ali
5. a. Secretariat
6. d. Soviet Union
7. c. Jackie Stewart

8. b. Oakland Athletics
9. b. Pelé
10.b. Women's Sports Foundation

Sources:

- Olympics.com (1976 Montreal Games and Title IX)
- Baseballhall.org (MLB milestones)
- Formula1.com (championships and drivers of the 1970s)
- History.com (sports history and notable events)

1970s: Politics and World Events

Answers and Sources:

1. a. Watergate
2. b. Vietnam
3. c. Iran
4. c. Greenpeace
5. a. Watergate Scandal
6. a. Helsinki Accords
7. a. Angola
8. b. Afghanistan
9. b. Paris Peace Accords
10.b. Jimmy Carter

Sources:

- History.com (Watergate, Vietnam War, and global political events)
- Britannica.com (Cold War agreements and movements)
- Nobelpeacecenter.org (Camp David Accords and global diplomacy)
- Greenpeace.org (environmental activism in the 1970s)

1970s: Everyday Life

Answers and Sources:

1. a. Walkman
2. d. Monopoly

3. b. Adidas Superstar
4. b. McDonald's
5. a. Microwave oven
6. c. Atari 2600
7. b. Lava Lamp
8. c. Custom vans
9. d. Blow dryer
10. b. *Sesame Street*

Sources:

- Smithsonianmag.com (consumer products and household innovations of the 1970s)
- Britannica.com (trends and technological advances)
- History.com (pop culture and everyday life)
- Atari.com (history of home gaming consoles)

1970s: Business and Innovation

Answers and Sources:

1. b. Apple
2. a. Starbucks
3. a. Wendy's
4. a. Polaroid SX-70
5. c. Chanel
6. a. OPEC
7. a. Betamax
8. b. Walmart
9. a. The microprocessor
10. a. PepsiCo

Sources:

- History.com (founding of major companies and economic trends)
- Smithsonianmag.com (inventions and innovations of the 1970s)
- Britannica.com (energy crisis and global milestones)
- Intel.com (microprocessor history)

Bonus Round Answers:

1. b. *Schoolhouse Rock!*

2. c. *Star Wars*
3. b. Pet Rock
4. b. *Dungeons & Dragons*
5. b. Microsoft
6. a. General Electric
7. a. Opium
8. a. Hip-hop
9. b. Honda
10.b. The NYC Blackout of 1977

Sources:

- History.com (pop culture and historical events of the 1970s)
- Smithsonianmag.com (inventions and technological milestones)
- Rollingstone.com (music history and cultural impact)
- Britannica.com (emerging trends in the 1970s)

<u>1980s:</u>

1980s: Culture and Entertainment

Answers:

1. b. *E.T. the Extra-Terrestrial*
2. c. "Thriller"
3. b. *The Cosby Show*
4. d. Workout wear
5. c. Pac-Man
6. b. Madonna
7. b. *Back to the Future*
8. c. Cabbage Patch Kids
9. b. *Blade Runner*
10. c. *Thriller*

Sources:

- IMDb.com (movies and television of the 1980s)

- Rollingstone.com (music and album milestones)
- Smithsonianmag.com (pop culture of the 1980s)
- Britannica.com (video game history and cultural impact)

1980s: Cars

Answers and Sources:

1. b. Chevrolet Corvette C4
2. a. Toyota Corolla
3. a. Ferrari
4. d. DeLorean DMC-12
5. b. Mercedes-Benz
6. c. Chrysler
7. b. Lexus LS400
8. b. GPS navigation system
9. a. Mazda RX-7
10. d. Buick Grand National

Sources:

- Hotrod.com (iconic cars and innovations of the 1980s)
- Britannica.com (global automotive history)
- History.com (evolution of car features)
- Smithsonianmag.com (cultural impact of 1980s vehicles)

1980s: Fashion

Answers:

1. b. Power dressing
2. b. Nike Air Jordans
3. a. Jean Paul Gaultier
4. a. Lycra (spandex)
5. a. Mullet
6. c. Boy George
7. b. Ralph Lauren
8. b. Scrunchies
9. a. Gianni Versace

10.b. Rocker style

Sources:

- Vogue.com (1980s fashion trends and iconic designers)
- Smithsonianmag.com (cultural influence of 1980s fashion)
- Rollingstone.com (music-inspired fashion)
- Britannica.com (global fashion movements)

1980s: Sports

Answers:

1. b. Soviet Union
2. a. Steffi Graf
3. b. Michael Jordan
4. b. Tyson vs. Spinks
5. b. Florence Griffith Joyner
6. b. New York Mets
7. b. Hulk Hogan
8. a. Ayrton Senna
9. b. Los Angeles
10. b. Diego Maradona

Sources:

- Olympics.com (1980 Winter Olympics and 1984 Summer Games)
- Baseballhall.org (1986 World Series and MLB milestones)
- Formula1.com (Ayrton Senna and F1 history)
- History.com (1980s sports and cultural icons)

1980s: Politics and World Events

Answers and Sources:

1. b. Ronald Reagan
2. a. Fall of the Berlin Wall
3. b. Iran
4. b. Solidarity
5. c. Seven

6. b. Live Aid
7. a. Chernobyl
8. b. Glasnost
9. a. Nelson Mandela
10.a. Falklands War

Sources:

- History.com (Cold War and key events of the 1980s)
- Britannica.com (global political movements)
- Smithsonianmag.com (Chernobyl disaster and other world-changing events)
- Nobelpeacecenter.org (Nelson Mandela and global human rights movements)

1980s: Everyday Life

Answers:

1. b. Apple Macintosh
2. a. Walkman
3. a. Pringles
4. c. Donkey Kong
5. a. Friendship bracelets
6. b. Commodore 64
7. b. Nintendo Entertainment System (NES)
8. a. Cap'n Crunch's Peanut Butter Crunch
9. a. Polly Pocket
10.c. Jane Fonda's Workout

Sources:

- Smithsonianmag.com (consumer products of the 1980s)
- History.com (technological milestones of the 1980s)
- Britannica.com (video game and toy innovations)
- Rollingstone.com (pop culture and everyday life trends)

1980s: Business and Innovation

Answers:

1. b. Microsoft
2. c. McDonald's
3. b. AT&T
4. c. Casio Calculator Watch
5. c. FedEx
6. c. Lexus
7. b. Coca-Cola
8. a. Sony
9. d. Membership Rewards
10. b. Nike Air Jordans

Sources:

- Smithsonianmag.com (technology and business innovations)
- History.com (economic trends and product launches)
- Britannica.com (1980s brands and global expansions)
- Rollingstone.com (cultural impact of business innovations)

Bonus Round Answers:

1. a. *Tetris*
2. b. Dell
3. c. Live Aid
4. b. Rubik's Cube
5. b. Calvin Klein
6. b. Ronald Reagan
7. c. Nintendo
8. c. Statue of Liberty
9. a. *Pac-Man*
10. b. New Coke

Sources:

- History.com (key events of the 1980s)
- Britannica.com (technological and cultural milestones)
- Smithsonianmag.com (1980s consumer trends and cultural phenomena)
- Rollingstone.com (music and global events)